What people have said ab

Andrea Strachan

Fantastic book, couldn't put it down. It brought back many happy memories of my childhood growing up in Bonnyrigg in the 60s. Tears were rolling down my cheeks with laughter at many of the author's antics. The description of the burning down of the train station and the almost early unrequested cremation of a late client awaiting burial. I would thoroughly recommend this book.

Helen Renton

Really enjoyed this book, especially as I was growing up in the same place at the same time as Sandy. However, even if you didn't have this knowledge Sandy's manner of writing is so endearing it draws you right into his childhood. So pleased to have had the chance to enjoy this piece of magic.

John Ellis

A hilarious and poignant memoir that will appeal to anyone growing up in the world of the 1950s

Amazon Customer

A time machine that will make you laugh out loud. Being a late 70s child it's lovely how Sandy transports you back in time, to live life like your parents: he really makes you feel like you're there. You may cry, but you will definitely laugh out loud!

Margaret Sørhagen

Love your recollections Sandy. I also used the shortcut from school to the High Street through the' half-mile tunnel'. Marion and Jennifer were two of my companions through the dark tunnel. Sadly, neither of them are with us now.

Denise Thompson

Your stories brought back lots of memories of happy days at Lasswade Primary. Really enjoying your stories Sandy!

Helen Renton

Oh,. Sandy how I enjoy your stories! You are a very talented writer and as I am from the area and only a wee bit older than you, I can say with conviction how true your feelings and impressions reflect those of our generation during our childhood years.

Moira Kraweyzie

As usual, it's another enjoyable read Sandy. You must have quite a following from past school friends by now. It's good for us: the other contemporaries of that time, to be able to recognise names we also knew when we were of that tender age. I think your stories are good memory shakers and they get the old grey cells moving!

Denise Thompson

Your stories brought back lots of memories of happy days at Lasswade Primary. Really enjoying your stories Sandy!

Barbara Gould

Really enjoyed reading your book. Bringing back so many memories.

MEMORY SPILL

A memoir of a boy growing up in Bonnyrigg, a small town near
Edinburgh in Scotland. The story begins in 1953… Humorous,
slightly irreverent and sometimes poignant.

Sandy Wilson

CHEVIN
Manuscripts

Lyrics from 'Big Rock Candy Mountains': Burl Ives
Lyrics from 'Ging Gang Goolie': Lord Baden-Powell
Lyrics from 'When a hearse goes by': No idea

A CIP catalogue record for this title is available from the British Library.

ISBN   978-1536958409

Cover design

Andy Driver of AddCreative designed the book cover. Andy is a graphic artist and website designer. www.addcreative.co.uk

The Author

In 1970 Sandy Wilson completed his educational journey at Napier College of Science and Technology, then, as an eager Interior Designer, he emigrated from Scotland to England in search of work. There, Sandy astonished a group of his new Sassenach friends when he cheered, and fist pumped as Domarski scored for Poland to end England's slender hopes of appearing at the 1974 World Cup. They had no idea that the Scots were like that.

Over the last forty years or so Sandy has moderated his behavior; softened his accent and adapted to his adopted country. When he takes his dog Poppy out for a walk, Sandy's wife Val, just like his mother would have done, turns down his collar, straightens his jacket and checks his fly is done up. She would, if he had any, comb and smooth his hair.

This book is dedicated to my parents
Jim and Nell Wilson

Authors note

This is the second edition of Memory Spill. Last year I was asked to make an audio recording of my book for Midlothian News and Views Talking Newspaper. Apart from realising that I sounded like Andy Murray impersonating Darth Vader I noticed, while reading out loud, that there were quite a few errors, grammatical slip-ups and leaden prose. My English teacher 'Toy Balloons' would have had her head in her hands. I hope she would give me better marks for this edition.

Many readers corrected my memory of some of the people and events. For example: it was Mrs Cunningham, not Miss Neilson, who arranged for Mr Horn the missionary to show his film about Leopards. Sorry! Lepers.

Then Mike Strasser contacted me. He is the current owner of 119 High Street Bonnyrigg, my House of Memories. He emailed photographs of the house and garden as it is now. It was fascinating to see how the house and garden has changed. Mike sent me historical information about the house too. It seems that John Pennycook was the farmer who built the house, probably around 1750, in what was then called Bannockrigg.

January 2018

Contents

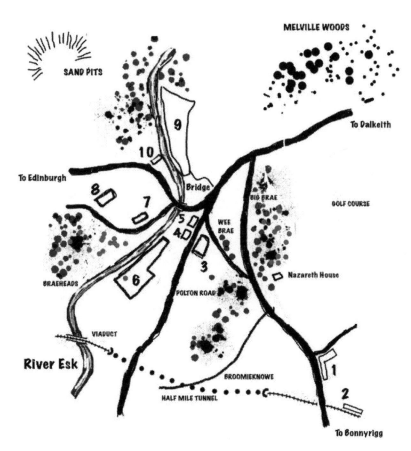

SAND PITS

MELVILLE WOODS

To Dalkeith

9

10

To Edinburgh

Bridge

BIG BRAE

GOLF COURSE

8

7

WEE
BRAE

5
4

3

BRAEHEADS

6

Nazareth House

POLTON ROAD

VIADUCT

River Esk

BROOMIEKNOWE

HALF MILE TUNNEL

1

2

To Bonnyrigg

1. House of Memories. 2. Broomieknowe Station 3. House of God 4. House of Ghosts
5. Post Office. 6. Paper Mill. 7. Wee School. 8. Big School. 9. Park 10 Scout Hall

The Village of Lasswade

I'll start here...

I was born in Edinburgh, the capital of Scotland and named Alexander. I was then, for the rest of my life, called Sandy. It is a Scottish thing. Just how Alexander becomes Sandy is difficult to work out. Difficult for me as a Scotsman, but almost impossible for the residents of England, the country where I have lived for most of my adult life. Invariably the English assume that Sandy must be the name of a dog or a woman. My elder brother was less fortunate. Christened William he was for the rest of his childhood know by the diminutive Willie. In his adult life, also spent mostly in England, he called himself Bill. But family and friends still know him as Willie.

A few years after moving to England my brother's name caused a public stir. One lunchtime, I met up with Ann, my late wife, in the spacious and busy reception of the company in Leeds where we both worked. We sat chatting while Ann leafed absently through a magazine. "Look at this picture! That looks just like your Willie" she exclaimed in the loud voice you use when something takes you by surprise. This sudden change in direction of the conversation wrong footed me, but not as much as the secretary, about to climb the nearby stairs, her files falling to the floor with a clatter, as she stumbled on the first step. The receptionist, on the phone, paused mid-sentence, and stared, eyebrows arched, across the top of her desk. For a few seconds the hubbub of the reception froze. The businessman sat opposite probably thought we were perusing a copy of The Lancet. But all that is a long way forward in time.

In 1955, I started at Lasswade Infants School; I was five years old. One of my earliest memories is of sitting at a wooden desk laboriously forming letters on a piece of slate framed with wood. It was about the same dimensions as the iPad tablet that a lifetime later I use to write, use to form my letters. How things have advanced in my lifetime!

This was the same school that my mother and her mother attended before me. The village I passed through on my journey to school had altered little; although in decline, the village still had a few of the shops that had existed at the start of the century, the parish church was still the social hub of the community and the paper mill still polluted the river. I had the privilege to live my early childhood when the pace of life was slower, more measured and required few props and gadgets to amuse us. But, the 'Swinging 60s' was just around the corner; the era of sex, drugs and rock 'n roll. The Cold War was in full swing, President Kennedy would be assassinated, Neil Armstrong would walk on the moon, an avocado bathroom suite was the ultimate interior design statement and we would all wear ridiculous flared trousers.

My memories, the primary source of the stories in this book, are often unreliable and questionable. Some, though, have been substantiated. Two years ago, I was astonished to receive an email from America. It started "Who the heck are you......" The writer, Janice Kos from Andover, Massachusetts had been searching the Internet for Tooter Ritchie, one of her classmates at Lasswade High School in the 1960s. Her search brought up a story I had posted on my blog. The story about a cricket match during a PE lesson at Lasswade Secondary School was true, but Tooter and Skud were probably not present. I just borrowed their names to give the story a bit of colour.

Margaret Duncan (now Margaret Sørhagen), who now lives in Norway, and Moira Grandison (now Moira Krawczyk) confirmed that the extraordinary leper story really happened, and my former classmates recalled with pleasure the songs taught to us by the American music teacher. Another contemporary, Christine Causer, contacted me to say she had been present at the scary séance held in the church vestry that cold November night.

I have described some teachers unkindly. Please don't take these portrayals seriously. They were good people and excellent teachers. But as a schoolboy my opinions of teachers mirrored my abilities, or inabilities to be exact, at certain subjects. I was useless at anything involving sport or maths, and so I loathed the teachers who were making their best efforts to educate me in those subjects.

Any grammatical errors simply confirm that I should have paid attention to what 'Toy Balloons', our English teacher, was saying in class; instead I was distracted, like most of the boys by her magnificent physical attributes.

I hope readers will enjoy my stories, find them amusing, but excuse the inaccuracies and the gentle vulgarity. What one of Nicola Sturgeon's 'Named Person Guardians', had they existed would have made of it all, God only knows!

Chapter 1
House of Memories

One of my first childhood memories is watching, fascinated by a plane, its turboprop engines thrumming in the air, as it rose into the summer sky. The silver fuselage glinted as it turned to disappear into the white clouds. Then I noticed the shadows, thrown by the wind-driven clouds, tumbling over the roofs of the nearby houses, running across the field and leaping the fence at the bottom of the garden. Then the dark angry monsters slid over the lawn towards me. I ran, frightened, into the house yelling for mummy.

It was 1953, and I was 3 years old. I lived with my parents and my older brother in a bungalow in Corstorphine, a suburb of Edinburgh, near to Turnhouse Airport. The air raid shelter in the far corner of the back garden dating the house as before the Second World War. A well-established Rowan tree with memorable cascades of orange berries, stood sentry at the front gate. My dad worked at a branch of the Royal Bank of Scotland somewhere in the depths of the city, and my

Memory Spill

mum, in the fashion of those days was a full-time housewife. She lacked training in the art of motherhood, her own mother having withdrawn from the world on the death of her beloved husband Clem, a casualty of the First World War. And so, I imagine my mother struggled to control her two young sons, given that one was an amateur pyromaniac.

One day, when she was having her habitual afternoon siesta, I was playing with my older brother in the air raid shelter at the top of the garden. The rusty corrugated tin that curved over a rectangular hole in the ground had a covering of turf to conceal the shelter from the bombers that would have circled overhead. A mound of earth encircled the entrance, to act as a blast wall. I doubt any of this would have saved the wartime occupants of 17 Castle Avenue from a stray bomb. We were play acting, mimicking war time activities we had seen in picture comics and stuff on the television that dad had bought to witness the recent Coronation.

I had crept out of the dank, musty air of the shelter to look over the earth mound for imaginary advancing German soldiers. I didn't see any Germans, but I noticed a ribbon of white smoke rising from the wooden coal bunker that leaned against the bungalow wall. I looked sideways at Willie who was lying alongside me. He didn't look concerned, even when the smoke was followed by a tongue of orange flame that licked hungrily up the wall to scorch the eaves.

Far away to our left, I could hear shouting and the clang and clatter of buckets. A tall, gaunt man, dressed in army fatigues, was running across the field behind our garden. We watched as, impeded by galvanised steel buckets swinging in each hand, he stumbled and staggered before attempting to hurdle the fence.

Our mother, roused from her afternoon nap appeared around the corner in a state of bewilderment, as our distant neighbour disentangled himself from the fence, crossed our lawn and threw the remains of the water in his buckets over the bunker.

The hero of the moment then sat on one of his buckets near the smouldering ruins of the bunker with his head in his hands, my mother having left the scene to bring a restorative cup of tea. My brother and I stood a few feet away, watching him in admiration, thrilled at the action and his war-worn khaki uniform. The poor sod was probably reliving a wartime trauma: storming Juno beach on D Day or charging across the desert, bayonet fixed, at El Alamein. Later, I listened as my parents discussed the event as though it was a random act of God or an example of spontaneous combustion. But I was certain Willie had something to do with the pile of charred timbers. Taking our role play too far, he may have imagined the coal bunker was a German pill box bristling with machine guns and he had vital orders to destroy it. He had achieved his aim. Field Marshal Montgomery would have been impressed and my brother would have been mentioned in despatches.

I have no idea why, but during my fifth year my parents put the house up for sale. It might have been to do with our next-door neighbour Mrs Williams, or the proximity of my overbearing paternal grandfather who lived not far away, or, in my mother's opinion not far enough away.

Mrs Williams, our neighbour was off her trolley. She was an amateur percussionist. Most afternoons she would manically beat all the pots and pans in her kitchen with a ladle. When the heavy metal cacophony broke out on the other side of the wall, our mother would call us in from the garden to watch Andy Pandy or the Flower Pot Men. On rare sunny days, our mad neighbour would put aside her kitchen utensil drum kit and ride a bicycle around her garden while dressed in an immodest swim suit singing at the top of her voice. Dressed in our more modest swimming trunks, knitted by our mother from patterns published in the Woman's Realm, we would peer through the hedge, transfixed by this strange performance.

Memory Spill

Then, our mother, shouting to make herself heard above the banshee, would call us into the house to preserve the remnants of our innocence.

Mrs Williams disappeared for a while and peace descended, like a soft blanket, over the neighbourhood. Then, one day Willie and I, sat on the wall of the front garden feet dangling, watched her arrive home in a black limousine. Her husband protected her tightly bandaged head as he helped her out of the car. Then, with the help of a small man in a white coat and round wire rimmed glasses, he led his bewildered wife towards their house.

The other reason to leave town was our grandfather. We knew him as 'Graffy'. A moniker that conjured in the mind a fond picture of a grandpa, slightly reeking of pipe tobacco, who would tell exciting tales, inappropriate jokes and play exciting games. Sadly, he had none of these attributes. Unbending and cantankerous, my mother detested her father-in-law, and I feared him. One morning, after an overnight stay with our paternal grandparents, my ablutions failed to meet Graffy's high standards. He marched me back into the bathroom and scrubbed my neck with my face submerged under water. I surfaced, sucked in a mouthful of air and soap suds before being dunked back in the sink. After this session of water boarding Willie packed our bags and sneaked us out the front door and headed home, only for our long-suffering grandmother to run after us and persuade Willie to bring me back to their house.

It was no surprise that my father had escaped from his childhood home in Portobello as soon as possible. He was employed at a branch of the Royal Bank of Scotland in Dalkeith, a town some distance away from his home and his father. In the town, he found lodgings and lived in a more congenial atmosphere with a pleasant retired couple. Over time he developed a social circle, encompassing the neighbouring town of Bonnyrigg and Lasswade village. He met

4

my mother at Bonnyrigg Tennis Club before the war and then when demobbed he married my mother at Lasswade Parish church.

All this may have influenced the choice of location of our new home. The house would stand among familiar haunts and be near to my mother's slightly eccentric, but good hearted, family. And so, with the bungalow in Corstorphine sold, we moved to Bonnyrigg, then a small industrial town about seven miles to the south of Edinburgh. The main industry was carpet manufacturing and the air for most of the week was tainted with the smell of jute that seeped from the factory just down the High Street from our new home. Below the town, nestled in the Esk valley, lay the village of Lasswade where my mother's family had lived for at least two generations. The water of the River Esk was essential to the paper mill that dominated the village. As part of the production process the water flowed into the mill at one end was then pumped back out as a foul smelling chemical cocktail in various colour combinations that swirled and joined the pollutants discharged by other mills further upstream.

Swapping a leafy suburb of Edinburgh for this reeking industrial environment didn't seem a sensible idea. I must have thought my father had taken leave of his senses. But, I felt I had arrived at a spiritual place, surrounded by benign relatives and shades of my ancestors. It was to be the start of a chaotic but happy childhood

Our new home, grandly named Hillhead House was part of a jumble of buildings that had long ago been a farm before being absorbed into the town. Our portion of the house was part of what would have been the farmer's house and included the some of the ground floor and two rooms to the front of the first floor which looked out onto the street. The rear part of the upper floor which looked over the back gardens was owned by

Memory Spill

Mrs Ferguson, who had connections with the Massey Ferguson tractor company and lived in a nearby mansion. Her chauffeur and his family lived in Mrs Ferguson's portion of the property. Attached to the main house and draped down the High Street were two cottages. The layout of the back gardens matched the hodgepodge of the buildings and resembled disorderly allotments.

We arrived on a bright spring day, the trees across the road casting deep shadows. It would be a hot summer that year. We waited in an excited cluster behind our father as he grappled with the unfamiliar locks then, as he pushed the heavy door open, I entered the house in the wake of my parents and brother. I had no idea what was going through their minds I but I was desperate to explore my new home. Behind the gloss painted front door there was a vestibule with a glazed inner door and tiled floor. A decade later the Kirkwood brothers, who lived across the road and their friends, would roll a large snowball into this small space leaving it wedged there for my brother and I, supervised by our annoyed mother, to push it back out onto the snow-covered pavement.

The inner half glazed door opened into a hallway with a stairway at the far end which curved up to the first floor, an amateur attempt at elegance, by the farmer who had built the house over a century before. Over the years, the bottom of the stairs would be the setting for many photo shoots: my parents in their evening clobber on the way to a bank function; my brother and I dressed as pirates for a fancy-dress party or looking smart in our school or scout uniforms. One year my dad, a frustrated engineer, built a working model mountain cable car up the stairwell built of Meccano and 'string. It impressed us, but not our mother as she negotiated the structure on the way to the bathroom.

My explorations would take me up the stairway later, but first I began a tour of the ground floor. The living room

Memory Spill

where we would sit, gathered around the small television set watching Wells Fargo, Bronco Lane or Dixon of Dock Green. If the TV wasn't on we would play Ludo or cards on the coffee table dad had made at night class. The table top, a mosaic cut from vinyl tiles had a chess board in the middle. When I was older, my father would teach me to play chess with ivory figures brought back from Egypt where he had served in the Royal Artillery during the war. At Christmas time there would be a tree in the window decorated with baubles, tinsel and unreliable coloured lights and dad would drape coloured crepe paper decorations from the 'Big light' across to the ceiling corners. Sometimes, like Victorian families, we would gather around the upright piano as mum played carols while my dad caterwauled on an ancient violin, accompanied by my brother and I blowing on combs wrapped in Izal toilet paper: home-made kazoos. Had we still been living at Corstorphine, Mrs Williams could have popped around to join us with her colander and saucepan drum kit.

I looked round the door into the bedroom I would, at first, share with my brother. Not long after moving in, I sat on one of the beds crushing a model Sopwith Camel biplane. It had been a gift to Willie from our uncle Al, who before he retired had been the restorer of artefacts and model maker at Chambers Street Museum in Edinburgh. The biplane had modelled superb authentic miniature details. When I lifted my arse, it resembled a miniature authentic air crash. My brother was angry, really angry. Years later, in my twelfth year I would sit on the same bed in stunned disbelief, after being told, on the way home from Scouts, that President Kennedy had been assassinated.

Moving on through the house I discovered the kitchen; a long rectangular room with a window looking out onto the chauffeur's garden. On the left of the window there was a cream coloured Rayburn stove. This heated most of the house and in winter dried our coats and boots. Often, we watched as our mother poured batter onto the hot plates to make small pancakes which we would spread with butter and jam and eagerly devour. During the demolition of Lasswade Old Parish Church was demolished dad bought some redundant pews. Using the skills learned at night class he adapted the pews to create a banquet dining area in a corner and a bench in front of the stove. During winter, in our teenage years, Willie and I and our friends would sit round the warm stove listening to Top of the Pops, playing poker, telling jokes and farting while our parents sat in the lounge oblivious of the commotion in the kitchen.

From the kitchen, a narrow passageway led to what we would refer to as 'down the back', an odd wedged shaped room. Today it would be called the utility room. At the back of this room a door opened into the garden. I found my mother and father standing deep in conversation. They were looking at a bath which stood in the room like the stranded hull of a small boat. They were wondering why on earth the bath was there? I too, even as a five-year-old wondered. Once the bath was installed in a more sensible location upstairs 'down the back' became a workshop where dad would potter about and where my brother carried out many of his devilish experiments.

Leaving my parents pondering the bath question I set off back through the maze of corridors to find my brother. I climbed the elegant stairway to the first floor. Facing me at the top of the stairs was a cupboard, then to the right a corridor which led to two bedrooms. I found Willie looking out of the window in the bedroom at the end of the corridor that would become the bathroom, a more suitable location for the stranded bath.

Clattering along the bare floorboards we returned to the top of the stairs and opened the cupboard to find a pith helmet lying on a shelf and an air rifle leaning on the wall. We carried our treasures back through the warren of corridors

Memory Spill

intent on exploring the rear garden. This was a jungle of long unruly grass hemmed in on one side by a tall rebellious privet hedge and a high stone wall opposite. The unruly garden sloped away from the house. In time it would be tamed and landscaped by our parents. But today, our first day of occupation, my brother and I stood at the back door, me wearing the oversized pith helmet and Willie with the gun in the cook of his elbow. Two big game hunters on safari, surveying our new domain: Hillhead House, still and quiet, waiting to be filled with our memories.

Memory Spill

Chapter 2
Infant School

At the end of the summer of our move to Bonnyrigg I started at the school in the nearby village of Lasswade. From our new home I would walk, with my brother, in the opposite direction to the town centre, then descend a rough track called the Wee Brae. From the bottom of the Wee Brae we would cross Polton Road and head down the Post Office Steps to the bridge that spanned the River Esk, a river that looked as though its contents had originated in Chernobyl.

We would cross the bridge and walk along the road that ran parallel with the river. Willie would leave me at the Infant School then make the steep climb up the School Brae to the Primary School. The Infant School, behind the church hall, was a recent building whereas the Primary School was a Victorian pile at the top of the hill which our mother and her mother before her had been pupils.

Memory Spill

The Infant School was a long two-story structure with most of the classrooms on the top floor reached by an external broad stairway. In front of the building there was a wide tarmac covered playground with a low wall to one side. On the other side of the wall there was a dangerous long drop into the gardens below. Willie McRob showed how dangerous by somehow toppling over into a garden. Hearing his cry of alarm, we left our games and gathered at the wall to look down at our fallen classmate. A bed of colourful summer blossom had cushioned his fall. The homeowner was looking up, a thespian in a Shakespearian play sweeping his gaze over the audience of small pale faces in the upper circle.

He was struggling with conflicting emotions; astonishment at the sudden appearance of a small boy in his garden, concern about the boy's wellbeing and disappointment at the decimation of his much-admired dahlias. Mrs Blair, our teacher, arrived and pushed her way to the front row while another teacher shooed us away. Willie survived the fall to reappear a week later, with a swagger, sporting a turban of white bandages.

I was about to have an accident of a different sort. Still coming to terms with school life, I was sitting, somewhere in the middle of the classroom, at a wooden desk, one in a regimented sea of desks. The sun streaming through the large windows, washed over the heads of my fellow pupils, making the room stiflingly warm. We were being taught the rudiments of writing. Forming the basic letters with chalk on small rectangular wooden framed pieces of slate, the chalk screeching as we painstakingly drew the letters while the teacher patrolled the classroom.

My mind was elsewhere; mulling over the latest exploits of Davy Crockett or Quatermass, a scary science fiction TV film which surprisingly my dad had allowed me to watch at the impressionable age of six. Then, I became conscious of the class stirring in a state of mild excitement.

Memory Spill

Our teacher had announced that we were about to go to our music lesson in the gym at the far end of the school where I would clumsily wield a triangle, the extreme limit of my musical talents.

As we waited in the classroom, my day unravelled with an unexpected and uncontrolled fart. As the music lesson was in the offing, it had an appropriate melodious tone, but it was loud enough for Mrs Blair, a middle-aged teacher with grey permed hair, to give me a disapproving look, and the girl sitting next to me to snigger. Looking down at the top of my ink stained desk I studied the array of names scratched by former pupils. I was no longer anonymous; I was the centre of attention.

The moment passed, and I slipped back into my default daydreaming mode. But this didn't last long. There was an uneasy awareness that the smell of poo was smothering the room.

My recent fart put me in the frame as the source of the smell. Mrs Blair, suspicious that I had suffered a catastrophic 'follow through' told me to move and sit at the front of the class. I sat there with a red face, the teacher leaning over me, her nostrils flaring. She was probably toying with the idea of opening the windows; weighing up the benefit of releasing the poo smell against allowing the ever-present chemical odours wafting from the paper mill to enter the room. The smell of shit persisted. Things for me were about to get worse.

Memory Spill

As we left the classroom, the teacher marshalled the class into a column of pairs. Boy and girl holding hands. The teacher, casting me a stern look, cut me out of the milling herd and made me stand beside her. Under a cloud of intense poo smell the column started the march down the long corridor, our summer sandals squeaking on the polished parquet floor. It was as if the school sewer had fractured.

I stared at the floor as I walked holding hands with Mrs Blair. My classmates smirked at my discomfiture as the teacher stopped at frequent intervals to bend over, pull up the leg of my shorts with the fabric gripped between her pinched fingers and sniff, like a Chef de Cuisine lifting the lid of a pot to inhale the aroma of an uncertain culinary concoction.

The intense humiliation was short lived. As we neared the end of the corridor a girl in the column burst into uncontrollable tears. My humiliation was transferred from me to her as our teacher, with her long fingers, lifted the hem of her skirt to reveal a memorably large jobbie slung in her navy-blue knickers. The teacher removed the unfortunate girl from the column and, with no apology for being suspected of responsibility, I was told to take her place. I gripped the limp, reluctant hand of my new partner, a scowling boy. I was not sure what he had to scowl about; his last partner must have been a big disappointment. The column squeaked back into action and we headed towards the gym and, our music lesson.

I took my position at the back of our miniature orchestra, anonymous again, and tried to concentrate on when, during the cacophony of noise, to hit my triangle with the short metal stick. While I wouldn't learn much about music, I knew I had just been taught one of life's valuable lessons: never, ever fart in public. At least not loudly.

As the seasons passed my letters improved, but it was dawning on me that arithmetic would not be my strong suit. I

Memory Spill

had settled into a life of plodding learning, relieved with visits to my granny's house in the village as I tramped to and from school. A house of ghosts.

Memory Spill

Chapter 3
House of Ghosts

It was a short walk from the Post Office to the address on the telegram. Rather than send the boy he decides to deliver this bad news personally to his friend. At the door, he pauses to look up the familiar street, peaceful in the late spring sunlight and tries to remember, to recall happier times. He knocks, listens to the footsteps approach along the hallway he knows well. The door opens. He is relieved that it is Alex.

"George," says Alex looking at the small square telegram offered to him by the Postmaster.

Alex's reluctant fingers fail to grip the telegram which flutters to the pavement. He bends down to pick up the message of death; his three sons are in France, in constant danger. As he stands up their eyes meet.

"It's for Laura," says George. "It's addressed to her."

"Clem, then," says Alex, his mind a confused maelstrom of emotion; guilt at the good news that his sons still

Memory Spill

live battled with the grief that his daughter's beloved husband's name would be written in dark ink.

Then, a voice behind him breaks his train of thought. Breaks his heart.

"Faither, what is it? I heard Clem's name......."

Alex turns around to face his daughter, reaches out to catch her as she falls, her life, her future slipping through his fingers.

This is how I imagine the scene when the Missing in Action telegram was delivered to my great grandfather's house, 10 Polton Road. It was the pivotal moment in my mother's family's history. Five years later Alex would die of a heart attack. And his daughter, my granny, Laura, would retreat into a permanent state of grief.

Missing life

Beneath time swept landscapes
Where lost souls tread
You lie buried
Missing presumed dead
Your lost treasures

Memory Spill

Your future life
Your dreams
Entombed
No pale stone
No chiselled name
Marks the place
A passive poet
An uncertain warrior
You died young
In a holocaust made by men
Your beloved wife and child
Forever haunted by never
Healing sorrow and unfulfilled
Dreams of what might have been.

When the war ended one of Clem's comrades visited Laura to tell of how her husband had been wounded during the battle. His hip shattered he had been laid in a shell hole for shelter until he could be recovered. He was never found again and presumed dead in February 1918. One of 36,000 dead at Arras.

All this happened long before I came on the scene. Granny's house, a mausoleum of wrecked dreams had not changed in almost thirty years. Standing opposite the village Parish Church it was on my route home from school, a base camp before the steep climb home up the Wee Brae. I would call in, to scrounge pocket money or just hang out with the remnants of my mother's family; my granny, her sister Jen and brother Harry. Uncle Harry was the Office Manager and Company Secretary at St Leonard's Paper Mill, Granny had her war widow's pension and Aunty Jen didn't seem to work at all.

Memory Spill

My mother's family had lived in Lasswade for generations. Long before the First World War my maternal great-grandfather had run a successful, upmarket, painting and decorating business from the family home. Long before the 1950s, the business had folded. My grandfather, the driving force, had died, and with his demise, without his hand on the tiller, the business could not weather the economic storm and social upheaval that followed in wake of the First World War. But the family house, 10 Polton Road, remained, like a ship, washed up on a reef, the surviving bemused crew stranded on board.

The front elevation of the house had a large window which in the heyday of my great-grandfather's business, would have had arrangements of wallpaper and fabrics displayed to entice passing potential customers, but now was an empty void. To the right-hand side of this window there was the door into the shop.

A matching door on the left led into the house. On my visits, I would walk through this unlocked door, a portal into a lost world, run across the small square hallway, avoid tripping on the rag rug, and jump down the two steps to the dining room. If granny or aunty Jen weren't there I would walk through to the kitchen, a long stone paved room with a bath along one wall under a removable worktop. Ancient ringers and wash tubs still used stood against the opposite wall. Then, continuing my search, I would open the door in the far left-hand corner and look in the garden at the side of the house where a path led to the outside lavatory. If, when I located the two sisters, and they were busy, hanging washing out or gardening, I'd set off to explore the house.

There were two doors in the dining room that connected the living area of the house with the disused decorator's shop. One opened into the customer area, the other into the space behind the serving counter. I would often wander around the shop in the dim light that passed through the grimy glass of the shop window. I peered into drawers and musty cupboards. Tried on the tin helmet with the words 'Air Raid Warden' stencilled across the front. Play acted with two old rifles propped against the wall and look at the Special Constable's uniform I would, years later, wear at a Church fancy dress football match in the park.

While I rummaged around, I could feel the ghost of my great-grandfather, Alex. He was standing behind the polished mahogany counter watching the apparition of his wife, Ellen, bringing tea and biscuits for a customer. A lady perhaps, from one of the large houses or villas that stood on the edge of the valley, above the village and high above the industrial stench from the river. Setting the elegant tray on a side table she would pour the tea. Then leafing through the large sample books, she would help the customer select wallpaper for her drawing room. Marvelling at her cultured Kent accent, my great-grandfather may have remembered how he had met her when visiting a stately house in Bexley in Kent. She the family nanny, he the assistant to a Senior Designer who was advising the house owner on the decoration of some rooms.

Leaving the shop, and taking leave of my maternal great grandparents, I would wander through to the entrance hall and climb the stairs to the first floor, walked past Uncle Harry's bedroom and into the drawing room.

21

Memory Spill

Like the shop, it had remained untouched since the end of the First World War. Unseen by me there may have been other shades of the past. My granny, still living, but whose soul had died along with her husband when he perished at the Battle of Arras, would have sat, chastely holding hands with my grandfather Clem on the settee in front of the elegant fire place. They were betrothed, and her brother Al may have sat on a chair opposite, acting with some reluctance as a chaperone, as would have been proper in 1912. Al and Clem were best friends, Al the artist and Clem the writer. They may have been talking about Clem's plan to join his brother Richard in Los Angeles to establish a publishing business.

As the ghosts of my family conversed, I would walk in the sunlight around the richly decorated room. My steps cushioned by fine rugs as I examined the ornaments, the bright brass Russian samovars and oriental ceramics and look at the watercolour and oil paintings set in tasteful gold frames. My great-grandfather in his lifetime had assembled a treasure trove of art and artefacts.

Then, hearing Granny calling me, and I would leave my ancestor's ghosts and clatter down the stairs. In the dining room, I might sit at the table, drink a glass of milk and devour an unhealthy plate of Scottish pink and white iced cakes, and listen to Aunty Jen tell stories, fictional or historical tales of the village; tales of medieval monks and Roman legionnaires; or if

22

everyone was busy read the cartoons from the Sunday Post: The Broons, Oor Wullie and Nero and Zero. If I grumbled about some teacher, horrible arithmetic homework or abuse by another pupil, Granny would shake her head and speak her standard homily: "Och, Sandy, life's a sair fecht." For her, life had been a hard fight, ever since her beloved Clem had vanished into the mud of the Battle of Arras in 1917.

My eternally mournful granny and my odd, emotionally detached uncle were casualties of the Great War. My granny robbed of her beloved husband Clem, and Harry, like many surviving soldiers damaged beyond repair.

One day, when I was about ten years old, Uncle Harry found me in the old shop where, to my joy, I had discovered leather bound volumes of a magazine published during the Great War. Each volume had superb illustrations and sepia photographs of soldiers fighting in the trenches, huge Dreadnought battleships ploughing through heavy seas, dastardly Zeppelins floating high over London and biplane dogfights. I was so engrossed in the books I didn't hear him come in.

He sat down next to me and began to talk about his war experiences. I felt a sense of embarrassment. Uncle Harry hardly ever said a word to me. He told me he had been a machine gunner in the trenches and how he had been trained to ensure the trajectory of the bullets would be high enough to hit the chests of the advancing Germans. Too low was no good at all, he said, as hitting their legs didn't kill them or would miss altogether; Harry sat beside me, a farmer instructing an apprentice in the art of scything corn.

He stopped talking as if his recollections were too much to bear. For a few moments, he stared across the room at the far wall, staring across his own desolate no-man's-land. He reached into his pocket and took out a handkerchief to dab his eyes. Then in a sad silence he got to his feet, gave my

Memory Spill

shoulder a squeeze, and left the room taking with him the ghosts of the German soldiers he had slain. A killing machine at eighteen, it was no wonder that Uncle Harry was slightly unhinged.

In the late 1950s Uncle Harry won the Football Pools. He had the cheque framed, and it hung incongruously among the other pictures. The sum he won, £900, was a substantial sum of money in the 1950s. Typically of my Uncle there was no celebration of the win or evidence of the money being spent. An indoor toilet or even a bathroom to replace the bath-kitchen would have been a good investment and made for a more comfortable life for his family without making a noticeable dent in his winnings. He prudently invested the money and the loo at the bottom of the garden, a cold draughty museum piece, was still there when the house was sold.

The war had not just left psychological scars, there were physical reminders too; a German bayonet displayed on a table, a helmet hanging in the old shop and bullets. Willie and I found the shiny brass bullets rolling about in the drawer of a dresser. I watched with a sense of foreboding as my brother slipped a couple into the pocket of his flannel shorts. Later, at home as I walked through 'down the back' on my way out, I passed Willie leaning over our dad's vice. I stopped and looked over his shoulder. He had one bullet gripped in the vice and he was about to hit the end with a hammer. I looked in alarm at the possible trajectory of the bullet. Had he managed to fire it the bullet would have passed through the window and taken out one our neighbours, or worse, someone walking up the High Street. The local police would have had a Midsomer Murder mystery on their hands. Old Mrs. Fisher, who lived in one of the cottages, had complained to our father when she discovered an air gun dart imbedded in her garden bench, where she would often sit enjoying the late afternoon sun. If she thought a small dart was a nuisance, a bullet would come as a nasty surprise. At 8 years old I didn't feel it was my position to mention the possible consequences of my elder brother's latest experiment and retreated down the garden to get my bike. I pedalled furiously down the High Street, keeping my head down waiting for the sharp crack of a gunshot.

As a child, I was unaware of the oddities, and the sadness that pervaded my granny's house; it was a harbour, a port of call on my journey to and from the village school. Soon, I would finish my time at Infant School and follow in my brother's footsteps and make the long climb up the school Brae to attend the Primary school.

But there was one member of the family who survived the war and escaped from the House of Ghosts: Alec, the eldest son of Alex Lothian. When I was 15 years old, he gave me a picture.

Memory Spill

26

Chapter 4
The Picture

Uncle Al, Alexander Lothian, was the only sibling to escape the strange house: the house of ghosts. The eldest son, he married in 1912 and served in the Great War, surviving unscathed; unlike his great friend, my grandfather Clem. Before he retired, ten years earlier, he had been the curator of the Chambers Street Museum in Edinburgh. He restored ancient artefacts, built fascinating working models and miniature ships, that I, as a child on visits to the museum with my father, would look at with my nose pressed up against the glass of the display cases. He was also an artist of great skill.

When we arrived in Bonnyrigg Uncle Al was living in retirement not far away, near the tennis courts. I would often call round to see what he was making in the large shed in his back garden. One memory is this:

Memory Spill

It is 1960 and I am 10 years old. I have called to see Uncle Al who is busy in his workshop, a long wooden shed set in the garden behind his bungalow. I open the door and step into a world of familiar smells; the sweet smell of wood, pipe tobacco and the sour smell of wood glue. I sit on a high stool, amongst the dust motes that hang in the sunlight and watch my uncle. He is stooping over the upturned hull of a model ship, shaping it with a spoke shave, the metal blade making a dull rhythmic hiss as it carves through the wood. Near to me, on the workbench, there is a completed sailing ship, a Man o' War, that seems to float on a sea of curled wood shavings, sails billowing with non-existent wind. A backdrop of small saws, chisels and files, the accoutrements of joinery, hang orderly on the wall.

Leaning against this array of tools is a small watercolour painting. Elbows on the bench, chin cupped in my hands, I look at the picture and ask where he painted it. He tells me it is a sketch for a much larger oil painting he has been commissioned to do for a wealthy

farmer. In the picture, a landscape, a small mountain stands under towering clouds with the farmer's fields and a copse in the foreground. Uncle Al, abandons his ship, to come and stand at my shoulder. He explains the composition, shares with me, his knowledge and his time. Later, I will see the completed oil painting, but I think it lacks the simple spontaneity of the sketch.

Days before my fifteenth birthday, I sat with my Uncle Al on the sofa in our lounge in the thin winter sunlight, as he taught me the principles of parallel and angular perspective, drawing elegant diagrams on a sketch pad. I carried this memory and used the knowledge throughout my career as a designer. At the end of this impromptu lesson he handed me a birthday present wrapped in brown paper. On the morning of my birthday I unwrapped the gift. It was the picture I had admire in his shed.

In the winter of the year he gave me the picture, Uncle Al died, closing the door to his treasure trove of knowledge.

Many years into the future, my mother would tell me how, after her father died in the First World War, Uncle Al, her mother's brother, became a surrogate father of sorts. In the Scottish tradition, I carry family names, like a line of wagons transporting the freight of family history into the future. The picture is signed with the initials and surname of my uncle: A. J. Lothian. Of my names, Alexander James Lothian Wilson, the Alexander and the Lothian are in honour of my mother's much-loved uncle. The name Alexander continues its journey as the middle name of my grandson Charlie.

Memory Spill

Chapter 5
Primary School

After an uneventful spell at the Infants School, I had made less than mediocre progress in anything connected with numbers, developed with my written work and showed promise at art. My parents seemed pleased. I sat with them listening to the teacher's appraisal, relieved that she omitted my misdemeanours from her assessment. In those days, a teacher would consider discussing the indiscipline of a pupil with a parent a poor reflection of their professional abilities. The pain of the belt across the palm or a piece of chalk bouncing off the forehead kept law and order in the classroom. So, my time in the Infants School had drawn to an uneventful close.

On my first day at Primary School I lined up with the other children at the bottom of the steps looking up at the soaring tall grey gables and peering into the dark entrance wondering what lay within.

Memory Spill

The school was a grey, austere two storey Victorian building with tall windows. On a dreich winter day, the building would not have looked out of place on a Hitchcock film set. It overlooked the village and stood well above the chemical stench of the river. It must have been there a long time; my mother and her mother before her had been pupils. In fact, it had once been a single storey building that had had an extra floor added.

When I reached the top of the Brae, I would turn right into the upper playground, a flat tarmac area that ran along the side and across the front of the building. Steps at each end of the front portion of the playground led down to two shelters, or sheds as we called them, which were open to the front with primitive toilets sandwiched between. The slopes to the sides of the stepped pathways leading to the sheds had a covering of threadbare grass.

At the clang of a bell wielded by a teacher we would line up at the bottom the steps that led into the dark interior of the school. There was a central atrium where we gathered for assemblies. Here we would sit cross legged on the polished parquet floor and listen to Mr Clelland the Headmaster inform us of school matters and announce church events and village affairs. One term started with a special assembly, convened to tell us of the death of our classmate Michael Bannerman. He had died in an accident during a summer holiday. Everyone knew already. I knew. In the cemetery above the school, I had been part of the Cub guard of honour at his funeral. In the hot summer sunshine, I had stood at attention near the open grave, a spectator at my first funeral.

The ground floor classrooms opened into the central atrium and the first-floor classrooms above accessed from a balcony. The stairway to the balcony had a steep polished mahogany banister which invited descent by the seat of the pants. One boy doing just that failed to notice Mr Clelland standing at the bottom of the stairs with a teacher deep in conversation. We watched as our angry red-faced headmaster pick himself up, gather his scattered papers together and march the unfortunate culprit to his office, a tight grip on his collar. We could almost feel the pain of the tawes.

All the classrooms were of Victorian proportions with high ceilings and windows with sills set at a height that prevented pupils, sitting daydreaming at their desks, from seeing anything but the treetops and sky. Teachers had a better view. Sat on a raised platform, intended to give a good view over the rows of daydreaming pupils, it also afforded a view of the surrounding scenery.

I enjoyed the informality of the art class and I was competent at writing. One of my stories won a competition organised by Cadbury's Chocolate. I received a certificate commending my submission and a gold foil wrapped Easter egg. Cadbury's, by organising the competition received atonement for saturating our bodies with sugar and rotting our teeth. While I could cope with art and English my numerical skills were being tested to destruction. The arithmetic calculations had become more challenging.

The imperial measurements and currency combined to produce mind bending exercises in the Arithmetic class. A perfect storm. Time would stand still as I sat staring at a question about a transaction in a curtain shop. Mrs McDonald would pop into Mrs Cameron's curtain shop to buy materials to dress her lounge windows. She required 13 yards, 2 feet of fabric at 3 shillings and 2 and a half pence a yard. Then to add to the nightmare she needed 4 yards of heading tape at one and a half pennies a foot. By the time she selected the curtain rails, that her husband Jimmy would fit that weekend instead of going to watch Bonnyrigg Rose football team, I was having a mental meltdown. The fictional Mrs McDonald may or may not have bought her curtain material for the correct price, but I couldn't give a toss. I was in Arizona riding alongside The Lone Ranger and his partner Tonto, my ten-gallon hat flapping down my back, wind rushing through my hair while firing my Winchester rifle at bandits or Apache Indians.

My father was an accountant in the Royal Bank of Scotland and he could run his finger down a column of figures and write the correct answer at the bottom. His youngest son was a big disappointment. I was a dunderhead. Dad would with commendable patience, try to improve my numerical skills with a pack of playing cards. Sitting beside him on the settee in the lounge I would attempt to add the numbers up as he dealt the cards onto the vinyl marquetry top of the coffee table he had made at evening class.

At school arithmetic seemed to occupy the whole of each morning except Friday mornings which were devoted to my favourite subject: Art. But there would be occasional relief from this bleak educational landscape of numbers. Numbers to be subtracted, divided and multiplied.

One day our teacher, Mrs Cunningham, announced with great enthusiasm, and to our unbridled delight, that instead of arithmetic we would watch a film about leopards. Mrs Cunningham was a devout lady and organised sparsely attended Scripture Union meetings at the school. She told us, in breathless tones, that the film was to be shown by Mr Horn, a *real* missionary from Africa.

I knew what a leopard looked like. I had seen a leopard close up in Edinburgh Zoo, peering dolefully, but menacingly at me through the bars of its cage, while I peered back feeling sad for the animal. A nature documentary wasn't my film of choice, but I was more than happy to about miss two hours of torture by multiplication tables. But this was not to be anything like David Attenborough on Zoo Quest.

We flooded into a classroom that had arranged like a small cinema. A screen stood at the front of the room and, at the back, behind the rows of miniature chairs, there was a

Memory Spill

large black projector standing on a table. The missionary, Mr Horn, looking the part in a pale linen suit, gave a short talk about the unfortunate lives of leopards and urged us to remember them in our prayers. I thought of the large cat I had encountered, imprisoned in the zoo and made a mental note to pray for it that night before climbing into bed.

The projector, with a sudden subdued clatter, burst into life behind us, throwing a cone of bright light across the dim classroom creating black silhouettes of children with pigtails and unruly hair, still Finding seats. Then, a small African village was large on the screen; round mud huts with thatched roofs scattered amongst palm trees. A haze of wood smoke from cooking fires cloaked the scene. It was theatrically sinister.

The audience stirred, and the small seats creaked. From somewhere at the back of the dark room a small voice called out, just audible above the tickering of the projector, "Ah cannae see nae Leopards, Miss!" My disappointed classmate would not see any leopards, but he was about to see a lot of lepers.

The camera panned around the village then focussed on a group of villagers. Beings, with grotesquely deformed limbs and faces were shuffling towards us through the thin wood smoke. The audience gasped, small bodies twitched, the seats creaked and scraped.

Memory Spill

We were silently absorbed by the horrific scene, the leopards forgotten. This was enthralling stuff. We were accustomed to this level of horror. Saturday matinees at the Regent, the local cinema, better known as the Flea Pit, served up, along with flea bites, two distinct film genres: The Wild West featuring men in big hats and six shooters chasing Apache Indians, or films set in the jungles of Africa featuring men in pith helmets who were carrying large elephant guns as they stalked slimy green monsters in murky lagoons. I imagined our teacher enjoyed a much more sensitive genre of film.

Mrs Cunningham, who must have taken leave of her senses to think a film about lepers was suitable for eight-year-old school children soon lost her senses.

"Oh no! Oh, god, these poor, poor people!" she gasped. Startled, I looked up at my teacher. She had her fist jammed in her mouth as she swooned and without a sound slid down the wall, taking a handful of our art class daubs with her. Then, as the cast iron radiator delivered the coup de grâce to the back of her head, she performed a slow motion sliding tackle on my chair. It was one of those ambiguous situations; funny yet serious. I lacked the life experience to cope. Taken aback by this sudden turn of events, I looked down at our stricken teacher, then turned to look along the row at my classmates to see, in the silent dimness, a line of pale faces reflecting my rictus grin.

The girls in the audience, displaying a sense of maturity beyond their years and way beyond that of the boys, took command. While I sat immobilised, entangled with Mrs Cunningham's sturdy legs, Gwendoline Criddle and Margaret Duncan rushed to aid our teacher to stand like indecisive paramedics discussing the crisis over her inert body. Then, the missionary, realising the inappropriateness of the film, switched the projector off, plunging the room into darkness. I sat in the murky half-light listening to our teacher's quick breaths and the slap of sandals in the corridor as Jennifer ran for help.

In the ensuing silence, one teacher shepherded us out of the classroom while another, assisted by Mr Horn wafted smelling salts under our teacher's nostrils. Mrs Cunningham was absent for a while and when she resumed her duties, there was no mention of lepers or even leopards.

School life drifted on. Grammar became more baffling, long division became longer and we would spend hours chanting multiplication tables. In our last year at the village school my class had moved to the more recent extension at the back of the school that overlooked the graveyard. From our classroom, we could see my family's grave stones and, high in the far corner, the lonely, brighter one marking Michael's resting place. In our last year, we distributed the free school milk. Pupils that performed well in the morning arithmetic sessions had the honour of delivering the metal crates containing the small bottles of warm milk to all the classes throughout the school. My abysmal numerical talents meant that I would never enjoy this perk. But there was one memorable episode in that final year. The American music teacher.

The American music teacher joined the teaching staff on a temporary posting. He stayed for all too brief a time; but for a short spell we sang exciting songs with wonderful melodies. Songs from another continent, another world.

Our usual music lessons involved stumbling through Gaelic songs about men cutting peat in dreich drizzle drenched glens or herring gulls soaring across dreich drizzle drenched slate grey seas. We had no idea what the Gaelic words meant; no more than medieval serfs understood Latin chants. Occasionally this dreary fare was lightened with jolly English ditties such as 'd'ye ken John Peel' and at Christmas, carols.

Memory Spill

The American teacher, with his rugged film star looks, brought to us hobo songs with lyrics that painted vivid pictures in our young minds; visions of box cars crossing vast foreign landscapes, tramps sleeping under canopies of stars, and cowboys roaming in places where the sun always shone. Songs with memorable titles; 'Hallelujah, I'm a Bum', which produced sniggers, and 'Big Rock Candy Mountains'.

Accompanied by Our American teacher on the school's ancient, out of tune upright piano we sang of bees in peppermint trees, of the place where lemonade springs and the bluebird sings. And, the hauntingly evocative 'Moon River' from the film Breakfast at Tiffany's.

My persistent hearing problems made me a less than enthusiastic participant; as in most classes I had a tendency to cause trouble. After one episode of misbehaviour the teacher banished me from the classroom to stand in the corridor; the last resort of exasperated teachers.

The corridor was a terrifying place to be. Mr Clelland, the headmaster, roamed the corridor; a super hero, his cloak flapping in his wake. His mission: to mete out punishment to any miscreant pupil he came across. In Scottish schools the tawes, a thick leather belt, was the traditional implement used to administer punishment by smacking the outstretched hand. The word smack doesn't convey the effect of being struck by the belt; the hand could sting for hours and worse if a myopic teacher caught the wrist. However, on this occasion my ordeal didn't last long.

Memory Spill

As I stood in terror looking up and down the corridor when the classroom door opened, and our American teacher appeared in front of me.

He seemed a gentle and kind man, so when he morphed into a Chicago gangster, grabbed me by my blazer lapels and hoisted me up against the corridor wall with my feet dangling in space I was shocked. In his slow American drawl, he advised me to stop being "a stoopid kid" and promised that next time he would give me "a mighty good whipping" followed by various other dire promises. But the kind, gentle eyes that looked into mine belied the threats spilling out of his mouth.

I have often thought of this episode in my childhood. It was not so long after the Second World War. Perhaps our kind and gentle American teacher had seen or experienced enough violence and cruelty on some dreich drizzle drenched battlefield to collude in the cruel and unusual punishments of the Scottish school system.

I returned to the class room to continue my music lesson. Chastened and relieved I joined in with a rediscovered passion. And so, my spell at primary school drifted to a conclusion to the singing of some old American classics.

'Oh, the buzzin' of the bees in the peppermint trees
'Round the soda water fountains
Where the lemonade springs and the blue birds sing
In the Big Rock Candy Mountains......'

Up to this point in my life I had never shown an interest in music. My accomplishments so far listed striking a triangle and releasing a tuneful fart in Infants School. But the brief passage of the American music teacher through our school with his

39

Memory Spill

American songbook changed all that. Music became interesting and thought I'd have a crack at learning the piano. A bit of extra-curricular learning.

My mother, suspicious but pleased at this development, booked lessons before I had a change of mind.

The local piano teacher was Miss Reid, an intense spinster of indeterminate age, bohemian dress sense and wild hair. She lived at the end of a pleasant tree lined street, her house standing amid colourful horticultural chaos in the shadow of the local Scottish Episcopal Church.

I arrived, crunching up the path to her door thinking a machete would have been handy and that Miss Reid might be up for a spot of gardening during the forthcoming 'Bob a Job' week. Miss Reid's sensitively tuned hearing must have alerted her to my approach, and the door swung open just before I had the chance to use the large brass bell pull.

"Good afternoon. You must be Alexander?" asked Miss Reid in a cultured Edinburgh accent. Thinking she was speaking tosomeone else I looked behind me. No one had ever called me Alexander since my Christening.

I followed Miss Reid into the hallway. There was a smell of furniture polish mingled with a slight hint of cat piss. I suppressed a sneeze. On one seat sat an elegantly dressed woman who regarded me balefully as she noticed the dried streak of snot on my blazer sleeve. Mrs Reid shooed her cat off the other chair, so I could sit. The sound of exquisite piano playing filled the hall as she opened the door to return to the music room. This maestro must be the offspring of the aloof lady, I thought. Then thought the pianist must be at least twelve. The music stopped. The lesson had ended, and Miss Reid ushered out a girl wearing a smug expression. She was at least two years younger than me. I knew then I was out of my league.

Memory Spill

Miss Reid then summoned me into her drawing room which resembled a Victorian stage set. Patting the piano stool next to her she invited me to sit.

"May I look at your hands Alexander?" she said, holding them gently like a palmist seeking an optimistic portent.

"My goodness, such large hands!" she exclaimed.

I gathered from her tone that this was not a desirable physical feature of a successful pianist. She then peered doubtfully at my fingers as though examining pork sausages on display in Mr Scott's grocery shop. Sausages well past their sell by date.

Releasing my disappointing hands, she enquired "So, Alexander, what sort of tunes or songs do you like?" I really, really, wanted to say, "Hallelujah I'm a Bum" which we had sung with the American music teacher, but decided it best to play safe. I thought of the tune my mother persistently practiced at home.

"Claire de Lune, Miss," I muttered. Miss Reid, surprised by this revelation, contemplated the picture hanging above the piano, lost for some time in the peaceful scene of sheep grazing in some highland glen.

As weeks turned into months, the lessons progressed in the way that explorers struggle across endless snow-covered landscapes. Miss Reid would welcome me at the door with a look of resignation and sit patiently with me at the piano. At first, I could follow the notes, each having a letter denoting which key to press, but without these aids I was lost. A sheet of music was as incomprehensible as the Rosetta Stone or Egyptian Hieroglyphics.

At our first meeting, during the reading of my hands, Miss Reid had omitted to mention the annual concert; a showcase of the talents of her pupils. Held in the hall of the church next door, attendance was conspired essential by the

Memory Spill

local music aficionados. But not by me. I had two serious handicaps; my piano playing was abysmal, and I suffered from stage fright.

Miss Reid, in the interests of production quality sandwiched my performance between the smug seven-year-old girl playing Chopin and an equally smug teenage boy playing Schumann. When I heard my name called I clumped up the steps and clumped across the stage, heart pounding, to the piano clutching my music book in my large, sweaty hands and porcine fingers. An ominous hush cloaked the audience as I poked and prodded at the piano keys. I did my best, made a fist of it; literally. Then, as the echo of the last discordant note of my mercifully short piece faded, I clumped back across the stage to polite, very restrained applause.

In my ninth year my hearing problems came to a head. One day my father while I was playing on the living room floor spoke from behind his Scotsman newspaper and I didn't respond. His fears were confirmed. I was practically deaf. This explained my patchy education and failed music career. I was probably suffering from 'glue ear'. Nowadays grommets would be the cure, but in 1959 the solution seems to have been removal of the adenoids and I was operated on in the November of that year.

Memory Spill

Our teacher, Miss Neilson, probably thinking of something to keep my class occupied, gave my classmates the task of composing letters which would keep me occupied reading them in hospital.

The letters written in careful copperplate script pencilled onto lined yellowing paper told of the goings on at the school in my absence. Miss Neilson didn't censor the letters which told, not just of school events, but of the occasional breakdown of discipline.

Brenda Ewing told me that new sums were being taught and that we could do our homework in ink. She ominously wrote that "the teacher said if we had a mistake in our mental we would get the belt." Hearing this could have caused me to have a relapse. Mental arithmetic, or any sort of arithmetic, was my worst subject. Morag, daughter of the Polish emigre known locally as 'Joe the Pole' twisted the knife of anxiety by revealing that the new sums involved multiplying by pound, shillings and pence. This revelation would have had me ringing for the nurse. She continued "Mr Clelland showed us some writing from quarter to three till ten past three." This was followed by, "gym with Mrs Mackinnon's class till four o'clock."

Michael Blair, and Elizabeth told me that my team The Rabbits were very proud of me. "You have earned thirty-four points for your team by yourself alone," wrote Michael. Elizabeth had signed off with 14 kisses. David, my team leader, confirmed that I was second in this test by scoring 34 out of 38 points and that we were "still on tapestries at Handwork."

There was more praise from William for my test score "I must say 'well done'." Worryingly William signed off with three kisses. Norma Goodall revealed that discipline was breaking down "every day someone is being put outside the door" then, teasingly will not tell me what my score was in the test, oblivious that everyone else has told me. She ended her letter with eleven kisses. I doubt I appreciated this sort of attention from the opposite sex.

John Steel told me that "David's letter has a surprise." Obviously, my stunning test score. Catherine told me that, "in History we are doing Margaret Tudor and James IV," then confirmed that teacher was in a bad mood but, worryingly added, "she is very angry with you." Betty, in her letter, breathlessly elaborated on the collapse of order in the classroom. "Robert and Gordon started a fight and Gordon was put in a corner and Robert was put outside the door," then reported more trouble "a minute ago Jennifer's desk was pulled out to the front and she was made to face the class." In her long missive, Betty describes Remembrance Day the previous Sunday. "It was cold standing at the monument. The Brownies, Guides, Cubs and Scouts were there." I would have been disappointed to miss the ceremony; the name of my maternal grandfather Clem was on the monument.

Michael Bannerman must have been in a different classroom. In his letter, he told me that "the teacher has been in a good mood so far and we have had a good time and teacher has done some of your Handwork." This was Michael who would die the following summer falling from a tree.

Robert, the son of another Polish emigre, had learning difficulties, and sang in class and could be disruptive. But he was accepted as one of us. His letter, although neat, rambled. "I hope you got one operation and not two or three or four or five of them."

Catherine Swan with a hint of envy told me that Margaret Duncan's writing was best. And there is some truth in this. Margaret Duncan, a tall girl, in her best writing reported that "the classroom is so quiet without you." Then, as though I would be interested, "Elizabeth has brought her doll Vicky to school, and it has a pair of long pants and a hat and a jumper which are red." Despite complaining I am always pulling her hair she awarded me ten kisses.

Jennifer, the naughty girl facing the class, announced in spidery writing that "the tea tickets for the sale are out and cost one shilling." Vital information for a 9-year-old boy lying in a hospital bed. Gordon sympathetically stated the obvious when he wrote "I don't think you would like an operation."

Kenny, a collector of wild bird's eggs, mysteriously asked "I hope you are not forgetting our motto 'Shoo'?" Then described how "Fatty was sitting on the wall and I just about pushed him over. I wish I was you." Was I a bully? Was Kenny implying that if Fatty, whoever he was, was sitting on the wall when I was passing, would I have pushed him over? Or, did he mean he wished he was in hospital and not at school? Happily, Barbara made me feel better by telling me "We miss your fun!" Oh, to be popular.

After a period of convalescence, I returned to school and life continued as before. We were being prepared was for Secondary School and P.E. had become more serious. One day we were introduced to high jump.

I joined the queue to leap over the metal bar suspended between two tall wooden posts. Margaret Duncan, in front of me tensed her slender body then, graceful as a gazelle, bounded towards the apparatus and slid over the bar, landing still as a statue on the other side.

"Next!"

I turned to look behind me. There was no one there, I was the last in the queue. Running forward I attempted to mimic the scissor motion of Margaret's legs. But I didn't have her legs nor her grace. I clattered into the bar and crash landed on the mat then stumbled back onto my feet to the titters of my classmates and a sigh of disappointment from the teacher whom I had almost head butted in the stomach.

Memory Spill

It was a portent of my future. Physical Education could be added to the long list of subjects I would underachieve in at secondary school, the next stage of my tortuous journey through the educational system. But, in the playground, the streets and the local woods we played games that required physical prowess and skill. Games that I could enjoy.

Chapter 6
Games we played

I felt a dull thump, a thwack on my back. I had taken a direct hit by a snowball. Dodging more incoming missiles we retaliated. The kids from Nazareth House on one side of the road and us on the other exchanged broadsides like passing Men 'o War, snow balls arcing across passing cars containing red faced angry drivers. Then the firing subsided as we moved out of the range of each other; the orphanage kids heading towards the Catholic Primary school in the town while we disappeared down the steep Wee Brae, treacherous after a snow fall, and descend to the village in the Esk Valley.

Our periodic spats had nothing to do with religious intolerance, we were just school kids in different uniforms. One Christmas my mother sent me to Nazareth House with some toys we had outgrown. I knocked on the huge forbidding door and waited on the step. The lock slid, a chain rattled, and the door creaked open. A nun's head appeared around the edge.

Memory Spill

"Yes, my son," she said in a genial Irish accent.

I explained about the toys.

"Well now, that is just grand, so it is."

As I passed the bag of toys to the nun I glimpsed the cold, austere hallway stretching back into the building. There was a deep silence. No shouts, laughter or chatter. None of the sounds of children.

"God bless you," said the nun. The door closed in my face and I heard the key turn and the bolt slide home.

As I walked down the long gravel drive, I thought how glad I wasn't an orphan. It was only later in my life, much later, that I heard reports, rumours of the abuse of the children by the nuns of Nazareth House orphanages in other parts of the country; women who had given their lives to Christ, sacrificing a life of motherhood to care for the children of others. No surprise, I suppose, that it all went wrong.

It was the late 1950s, a time of innocence and simplicity. The games we played at school and at home relied on imagination supported by nature's bounty.

In the winter months, snow, when it fell, was the main ingredient of fun. Snow ball fights on the way to school, at play time and on the way home. At the top of the School Brae, slides formed like glaciers and, to the cheers and laughter of children, even the occasional teacher could not resist trying a slide. Balanced precariously, arms outstretched, coat flapping and a briefcase in one hand they would slide like curling stones, towards the school entrance. Playing ended when the bell clanged, and we would form lines, under clouds of foggy breath, at the entrance doors. As we sat down to our lessons steaming coats, and mother-knitted scarves, gloves and hats hid the classroom. Beneath this embankment of clothes, shoes and boots like washed up boats stood in puddles of melting snow. The teacher would struggle to hold our attention as fat snowflakes cascaded past the high windows. All we were interested in was the next playtime.

At the weekend we would search sheds and garages for our sledges and drag them through the streets to the hill in the local park or the Broomieknowe Golf Course where the pin flags formed slalom courses. In 1962 during the protracted winter, we sledged during the Christmas holiday and then the Easter holiday in April.

Spring would arrive to chase the winter weather away. My mother, if she was alert, might catch me leaving the house to go to school with my hair uncombed and my clothing in disarray. In the vestibule, she would make me stand as still as a statue, while she combed my hair, straightened my blazer, pulled my socks up and wiped any residue of snot from under my nose. She would take a step back for a moment, appraising me with an indulgent smile, but narrowed eyes; a sculptor admiring a work of art they had just completed. Then, I would be shooed out into the street where, before I crossed the end of Golf Course Road, I would have mussed my hair, unbuttoned my vivid purple blazer and pushed my socks down to my ankles. I wanted to look like William, the child antihero of the Just William novels by Richmal Crompton, novels which I read and absorbed. Novels which influenced generations of horrid children. We called ourselves the Black Spot gang in homage to William's Black Hand gang, complete with a flag and password. My brother published a gang newspaper with a small circulation of three that reported on local issues and on our nefarious activities.

My mum can't have been paying attention on the day I went to school with my shorts on back to front. To my relief none of my classmates noticed either. Sat at my desk I had looked down to make the horrible discovery. I stuck my

Memory Spill

hand up and requested a comfort break and sidled out of the classroom under the suspicious eye of the teacher.

After I had disappeared out of my mother's view and disarranged my clothing and hair to my satisfaction, I waved to Mr Scott who was standing outside his grocers' shop on the corner. He peered at me through his round wire spectacles. On the cusp of amnesia, he was baffled who I was. Then a car would approach, and I would run and use Miss Meldrum's garden gate to lever myself off the ground as it passed.

This was a version of High Tig, a game you could play on your own, without or without a friend. The game had one simple rule: every time a vehicle passed you had be off the pavement. A wall or a step would do, or on this day Miss Meldrum's gate. She rapped on her window in irritation, but she was a nice lady. Miss Meldrum once invited my mum, dad and brother and me for a meal. The main course was hamburgers. We had never heard of hamburgers; fast food was still a long way into the future. We were agog when she told us she had lived in America and had been a personal assistant to some business mogul in New York; Miss Meldrum was not the dull spinster we all thought. We sat listening enthralled as she told us of her life in the city of skyscrapers, yellow cabs, Brooklyn Bridge and the Statue of Liberty.

In the upper tarmac playground, if the weather was fine, we would play Tig in small groups and, sometimes, the enmity between the girls and boys would melt away and a game of Chain Tig would develop. Chain Tig was a communal game where one child chosen to be 'het' (or 'it') would run around trying to catch someone. When they caught a fellow pupil, both would hold hands and try to catch someone else. At the end of the game there would be an extended snake of screaming children trying to corner the remaining boy or girl. A game would be popular for a time then, for no clear reason would fall out of favour and a new game. A ball would appear in the playground and with rules agreed, dodgeball would be trending. If teams were necessary for a game, the election of leaders would be on the grounds of peer popularity or simply through basic natural selection. One leader would step, heel to toe towards the other. The one whose foot overlapped the other had first pick. At the end of the selection process the unwanted kid, the fat one or shy one may have felt humiliated, but would soon forget as the game, whatever it was, got underway.

In wet weather, everyone crowded into the sheds at the bottom of the grassy slopes. In the boys shed, British Bulldog or Corner Tig would pass the time. British Bulldog involved hopping towards the opposing player, your arms folded in front, trying to knock him over. The winner the last boy standing; often the one with a secret streak of malevolent violence in their make-up. The rules of Corner Tig were that you had to run between the corners of the shed without being caught by the person who was 'het'.

During some weekends, we would harvest frog spawn from the local ponds. The spawn would be brought home in jam jars and poured into the white ceramic sinks that our dad had incorporated into his back-garden landscape layout. The spawn would evolve into tadpoles then became small olive-green frogs to be hunted to near extinction by Nicky, our grey one-eyed cat.

Spring, with a few false starts, would with painful slowness change to summer. In memory, imagined days of continuous warm sunshine and blue skies. There were sporadic outbreaks of warfare with the Nazareth House kids. The projectiles were now stones, not snowballs, and a lorry driver with his window down struggled to control his vehicle when a stone struck his head. This incident resulted in a severe clampdown by the police, the school and the orphanage and an armistice declared.

Memory Spill

The warmer weather would dry out the slope of the lower playground creating ideal conditions for our racing cars: Dinky and Corgi miniatures of Cooper-Climax, Maserati, Alfa Romeo and Ferrari cars. During playtime we gathered at the top of the lower playground and set our cars hurtling down the dusty slope. The winner was the car that travelled the furthest. After school we would sit at our kitchen tables stripping tyres from miniature military vehicles and trucks to fit them to our racing cars, trying different combinations of tyres to improve performance; seeking to enhance performance, to make them go further the next day.

We imagined we were Stirling Moss, Jack Brabham or Manuel Fangio. One day I watched a classmate 'Fangio' place his racing car on his desktop to admire its flowing lines or tyre combinations. Our alert teacher patrolling the aisles spotted this inattention to the lesson and pocketed the model car with one hand like a magician while slapping the back of 'Fangio's' head with the other. A painful experience without the protection of the racing star's helmet.

At some point the interest in racing cars would fade and marbles, pea shooters or water pistols became the new fad. 'Jerries and British' war game enactments were a popular boy's game, fuelled by the relentless diet of Second World War films or stories in the comics I would read in Mr McKenzie's barbers shop while I waited for a military inspired short back and sides. While we boys played with our toys, the girls played games that seemed to require far more skill.

Standing in a corner of the upper playground with Kenny Miller I watched, mesmerised by the girls skipping at the same time as singing. Sometimes two ropes spun at the same time with two girls hopping up and down together through the arcing ropes. Such coordination! Hopscotch, too, seemed to require a high level of dexterity well beyond any boy's ability.

As the bell tolled to call us to our lessons Kenny turned and grinned.

"Ma brother told me this joke," said Kenny.

"Go on then tell me!"

"Have ye heard aboot the man that wanted to change intae a woman?"

"No," I answered.

"He jumped off a cliff and landed wae a fud!"

When you know 'fud' is the Scottish vernacular for the female genitalia it is quite a good joke. When you are eight years old, it is side.splitting. We stood in line at the bottom of the steps, trying, with little success, to contain ourselves under the stern scrutiny of the teacher, looking down at us from above.

As soon as he felt we were ready, dad took us swimming one evening each week. In those far-off days, there were no local swimming baths, so we went to Portobello, the seaside resort on the eastern outskirts of Edinburgh. Dad would arrive home from work, have his tea, then we would catch a train at Bonnyrigg Station; the one we hadn't burned to the ground. The swimming baths were on the promenade and the pool used salt water pumped from the sea. My dad had spent his childhood in Portobello and the swimming baths were a regular haunt, probably to keep out of the way of his

Memory Spill

overbearing father. He and his younger brother Bill were excellent swimmers and Bill was a medal winner. Framed photographs on the foyer wall showed Uncle Bill with other members of the local swimming team, dressed in the 1930s swim suits holding medals and cups. We would never attain such heights of success, but we learned to swim well. Later, when the school organised swimming sessions at a private school in Musselburgh, I was one of the few pupils who could already swim.

One evening the trip to the baths only got as far as the end of the station platform when I had a carriage door malfunction. We had stepped up into the carriage and being last on I closed the door. I had reached out with my left hand to pull it shut while gripping the door frame with my right hand to stop myself falling out onto the platform. The door slammed shut, and I turned to follow Willie and dad but discovered I couldn't move. I realised then I was held back by my thumb which was trapped between the heavy door and the doorframe. There was no pain, and I calmly called to my dad and pointed to the problem. He, less calmly, yanked on the cord and the train skidded and clattered to a halt. The guard appeared, pounding down the aisle to open the door to release my thumb, and a wave of pain that swept over me.

Later at the surgery, when Doctor Somerville drilled a hole in my thumb nail and released the fluid, the pain vanished. He bandaged my mashed thumb and told me to wear a sling for a week. Brilliant, I thought as we walked home; I had a valid reason to be excused a long list of lessons. Arithmetic and Physical Education topped the list.

Halfway through the week as I sat at my desk daydreaming while my classmates laboured over some writing exercise I noticed my name being mentioned.

"Miss, Miss!" One girl had her hand up. "Sandy doesn't wear his sling when he's in the playground doing things!"

54

Memory Spill

There was a murmur of agreement from the girls and I received sympathetic looks of solidarity from the boys. I stared at the informer with undisguised malevolence only to be reciprocated with a smug smile. Then I became aware that the teacher's head had swivelled around, like the mid gun turret of the Lancaster bomber I had drawn on the cover of my jotter. Her dark eyes under arched brows were gunning for me.

"But, Miss," I stammered, "Doctor Somerville said it would be good to take my arm out of the sling. Occasionally."

"Well, Sandy, I think this is one of these occasional moments when you may take your arm out of the sling and do some writing!"

With a sinking heart, I pulled my hand from the sling and reached for my pencil. PE was the next lesson. I would have to admit that I was up to whatever horrible exercise was on the lesson plan.

To the relief of the teachers and pupils the holidays came around. We looked forward to days of building gang huts in Melville Woods, the Old Sandpit or up the Braeheads. At first our dens were rudimentary: the inside of a large bush with planks laid on bricks as seats. Then, as we grew older the structures became more sophisticated in the way prehistoric cave dwellers evolved into house builders. In Melville Woods we would design dens using branches, logs and rocks. We constructed our first huts on the forest floor then with more ambition we climbed into the trees to build among the branches. In 1962 we built our last gang hut. During that summer we were hanging out around the disused sandpit. We had found two large curved steel panels perforated with holes which we dragged into a strip of wood that ran along the edge of the sandpit. We laid the panels over a deep hole and covered the structure with turf.

Memory Spill

The structure brought back memories of the air raid shelter in the garden of our home in Corstorphine. It could have served a similar purpose. Late that October, with the world on the edge of a nuclear conflict we sat in our den waiting. The air raid sirens had wailed, and our school closed for the afternoon of the crucial day to allow us to go home and spend our final hours with our families. We knew how serious the situation was; we had read and seen enough fact and fiction. The Cold War era had spawned many novels and films with apocalyptic themes. The BBC did its bit by showing documentaries about what to do should a thermo-nuclear missile land in your neighbourhood. Comically, one recommendation was to hide under the kitchen table, assuming you still had a table, a kitchen or even a house. The air raid shelter in our back garden in Corstorphine we had played in wouldn't have been much use.

When we weren't building gang huts, we built bogeys. Good wheels were essential, and we would sneak through the council yard fence, like commandos, to steal pram wheels. Bogeys were cobbled together from wooden fruit boxes and planks. The larger pram wheels were at the back of the chassis with the smaller wheels at the front. Ropes attached, like reins, to the front wheels provided a primitive form of steering. Only the more sophisticated models had brakes. They were exhilarating and dangerous to drive.

One summer we went to the Regal Cinema in the High Street to see the film 'Geordie'. It told the story of a puny Scottish boy who took a Charles Atlas body building course and ended up throwing the hammer at the Olympics. My brother, influenced by Geordie, cobbled together a makeshift hammer from large bolt attached to a piece of wire. I watched as he spun around on the lawn a few times and released his hammer. Had it not wrapped itself around the telephone lines above the gardens it would have sailed over Mrs Fisher's cottage and landed in the street, killing a pedestrian or penetrating a car windscreen. We stared up at the improvised throwing hammer swinging like a pendulum from the entangled telephone wires and went in for tea. Later, in the evening, my mother, trying to contact Jimmy Muirhead about her bakery order was surprised to take part in a confusing conference call with the surrounding neighbours: Mrs Fisher, Mr Cook, and Jimmy Coull, a bohemian artist, potter and craftsman.

Often, on hot summer weekends, we would, as a family go by bus to an idyllic place called Flotterstone at the base of the Pentland Hills. The bus would take us as far as Milton Bridge and from there we would walk along a road that meandered through a wooded area. Hidden in the woods there was a ghostly, old ruined church set in a graveyard. There we would walk amongst strange gravestones covered in lichen, moss and carvings of skulls and crossed bones before walking on to Flotterstone. There we would enjoy ice cream washed down with sparkling lemonade drunk from coloured plastic tumblers, the fizz tickling our noses. From there we walked up the road towards Glencorse Reservoir then along a path that followed the burn to a field known as Daisy Dell. Here we would play hide and seek in the bracken and build dams in the peat brown water of the burn with rocks and divots and play in the massive pools we had created. Years later Flotterstone would become infamous when in the winter of 1985 three soldiers during an army payroll robbery were murdered in cold blood. In my memory, a paradise lost.

Each year, all too soon the holidays would end and as summer turned to autumn, we would again make the long, long walk to school, pockets bulging with conkers. At home, I sat at the kitchen table and bored holes through the conkers with a bradawl from my dad's tool kit. I threaded strings through the holes and tied knots. In the morning, I headed for school to smash an opponent's conker off its string. A win added to my conkers tally, an opponent's miss would cause painful knuckle injuries. There were rumours in the playground of fifteeners or twentyers, and of unscrupulous kids who marinated their conkers in vinegar or some other sinister substance to harden them.

One day I suffered a combined knuckle injury by conker and a stinging palm, the result of getting the belt. For at least a week, a group of us had been ringing the bell of Mr Towers flat and doing a runner. Mr Towers our teacher lived on the top floor of the red sandstone apartments at the end of Golf Course Road, just around the corner from my home. He could have walked to our house and complained to my father about his son's extracurricular activities, but then, in the late 1950s there was no limit to a teacher's jurisdiction. One morning, just after Billy Watt had almost broken one of my knuckles, Mr Towers called the bell ringers to the front of the class and gave us a lecture followed by a thrashing with the tawes, or the belt. My father never found out from Mr Towers and not from me.

As the dark nights set in we would, as a family, play simple board games like Ludo and Snakes and Ladders or watch TV programmes: Wells Fargo, Bronco Lane and Dixon of Dock Green. On the way home from school stealing apples from Mrs Clarks small holding was a popular pastime with the added thrill of being chased by her shaggy German Shepherd dogs.

Memory Spill

Then, as Guy Fawkes Night approached, our pocket money financed small arsenals of penny bangers and jumping jacks which we would use to terrorise the local citizens. It was time for my brother to dust off his chemistry set and plan his bonfire night spectacular. The launch of Willie von Braun's rocket.

Memory Spill

Chapter 7
Willie von Braun

On a cold October night in 1957 I waited with the small crowd gathered at the top of the Big Brae. The unpolluted sky sparkled with stars and planets like scattered diamonds on a deep black velvet cloth. Uncle Al, one hand on my brother's shoulder and used the stem of his pipe to point out the Milky Way, the Plough and how to locate Polaris, the Pole Star. While we listened to our uncle, our dad was in deep conversation with Keith Moncrieff and Rev Hutchinson, the minister. Standing apart, Uncle Harry, in his customary silence looked up at the sky. The cool night air smelt of smoke; smoke from coal fires, rising from the village, and smoke from the cigarettes and pipes that glowed in the surrounding dark. In the otherwise silent night we could hear the last bus growling, changing gears, as it negotiated the bend in the village below. There would be other watchers standing on high vantage points all around Bonnyrigg and Lasswade. Waiting.

Memory Spill

"There it is!" Someone shouted. "Look, o'er there, above yon trees."

A dozen faces, pale in the moonlight, looked across to where the anonymous pointing hand pointed. We watched in silence as a small bright speck emerged from the haze arc slowly across the night sky. There was an overwhelming feeling of wonder and excitement as we followed Sputnik, the first man made object in Space before it dwindled to nothing into the hazy horizon. We had witnessed the start of the Space Race, and my elder brother's fascination for rocketry. He too would aim for the stars.

Willie was an amateur mad scientist. A pyromaniac, as our mother once described him, in her Scottish lilt. He was the main suspect in the curious incident of the fire in the coal bunker that had leant on the back wall of our bungalow in Corstorphine. When we moved to Bonnyrigg, he would follow the bunker fire with a blockbuster sequel.

The town of Bonnyrigg had two railway stations. Dr Beeching, Chairman of the British Railways Board closed one and my big brother, Leader of the Black Spot Gang, would terminate the other. It was on an obsolete branch line that had once served the paper mills in the Esk Valley: Broomieknowe Railway Station.

Memory Spill

The catastrophe occurred in the late 1950s during a scorching hot summer. Each summer holiday we would occupy a different location, build a gang-hut or shelter, annoy people, play games and sometimes just sit around a camp fire. On this year, we were close to home, in residence in the wooded embankment at the back of the doomed station buildings. Beyond Broomieknowe Station the line passed through a tunnel to reappear in Lasswade, cross a viaduct and wind down the valley the end at the paper mill at Polton. The engineering was a formidable investment for a railway company to service a few paper mills. Improved road transport had made it obsolete even before the investors turned a profit. But, like all Victorian structures, the tunnel and viaduct would last long after the last train rolled. We would often walk through the dark, dank half mile tunnel as a shortcut to the village. It would come as a disappointment to the Victorian builders that the station buildings on the Bonnyrigg side of the tunnel did not enjoy such longevity.

On the fateful day, we had walked down the High Street to the railway bridge where a path descended to the station. There, a line of substantial buildings formed a backdrop to the long platform, the ticket office and waiting room and other offices. Behind the buildings there was an embankment where the trees and bushes had spread and grown untended and forgotten by the then owners, British Rail. We were about to put right this horticultural negligence.

Just before the platform we stepped off the path and slipped through the bushes into this jungle. In a clearing, we gathered together dead wood and twigs to construct a fire. Once the fire had been lit, we sat against the back wall of the station; my brother Willie and a mutual friend called Hallie. A fire had no practical purpose in the summer's stifling heat; it was just something to do, a centre point to the morning activities, a marking of territory.

Memory Spill

A jam jar full of a suspicious and smelly yellowish liquid appeared in my brother's hand in the manner of a magician. He claimed this would make the fire burn much, much better. Our father, who had been in his, more responsible youth, a King Scout, had drummed into us that we had to extinguish a camp fire properly before leaving a camp site. We, heeding his homily, had a ritual that involved standing around a fire, before going home, and peeing on it; a boy's thing. But all the piss in the town would fail to dampen down the coming inferno.

I'm positive that my memory is correct, and it was my brother that brought the jam jar containing the strange fluid; he had previous form for this sort of thing. Only weeks before he had stumbled, screaming, out of the utility room at the back of the house with his forearms alight like a Christmas pudding.

I was grateful for this distraction as I was being lambasted by my father. I had cleaned his bike and as a special service polished the saddle with dark tan shoe polish. Impressed with his spotless Raleigh bicycle he had thanked me for my efforts. He soon changed his tune when he discovered that the polish had transferred onto his light beige trousers creating a prominent external skid mark as he rode down the High Street. But, distracted at the horrific vision of his eldest son ablaze, the skid mark was forgotten if not forgiven. In a throwback to his army days, dad exclaimed: "Fucking hell!" I added these new words to my expanding vocabulary as I watched events unfold. Gravel hit my ankles, and pinged off the spokes of his bike as he sprinted, like Allan Wells, up the garden path, grabbing towels from the washing line as he ran past to dowse the flames engulfing his eldest son.

I slipped away as my mum and dad had a heated discussion over a pile of singed towels and my smouldering brother.

Memory Spill

But, to return to the camp fire. We were all enthralled, kneeling and standing around the fire as Willie unscrewed the lid of the jam jar and poured a small quantity of the yellow liquid onto the smouldering pile of twigs. There was a sudden whoomph! as a huge fire ball rolled passed our astonished faces and soared into the tree canopy, followed by our eyeballs as they swivelled upwards. We were mesmerised, but not for long. For the second time in a short space of time I heard the new and interesting phrase. "Fucking hell!" my brother screamed as he realised that he was holding a Molotov Cocktail in his hand. In an understandable panic, he threw the jam jar to one side, its contents spraying into the surrounding tinder dry undergrowth. We were now in the centre of a maelstrom of fire. We scrabbled through the bushes and ran up the path, then with surprising calmness and presence of mind Willie stopped us at the station gate, to make us walk with studied casualness up the road to our house, not far away up the main road. Before Hallie left us to go to his house Willie instructed us to keep schtum; if anyone asked where we had been to say we had been playing near the golf course.

Willie and I and walked into our house and sat at the dining table watching our mother looking out of the kitchen window as she prepared our dinner.

"Och, it looks like someone's having a wee fire. I hope the washing won't be covered in ash." She said, looking out across the roof tops at the rising smoke.

This was a wee understatement. Had we been living in Alice Springs and not Bonnyrigg, we would have been driving out of town in a station wagon loaded with essential possessions, trying to out run a bush fire. The cloud of dense smoke blotted out the distant church steeple and dimmed the sun sucking all the light from the kitchen where we sat around the table on dad's recycled church pews eating our dinner in uncharacteristic silence. Our mother oblivious to the missing eyebrows, singed fringes and the faint stench of an unknown accelerant listened to the distant clamour of fire engines bells.

Later, the catastrophe was on the front page of the Dalkeith Advertiser. Our father tut-tutted at this act of vandalism while poring over the pictures of the devastation and a grainy picture of a startled Mr Black, the local coal merchant and funeral director. The photograph looked like a negative print of a panda wearing a flat cap. The paper reported how Mr Black, now a local hero had prevented the fire from spreading to his yard which overlooking the station; a vast area of piles of coal and tanks of various liquid fuels. His valiant firefighting had saved his Chapel of Rest and prevented the early unrequested cremation of a late client awaiting burial.

The disused station platform had been a shortcut to the housing estate beyond and for a while the police were on the case. A police van would park in the station entrance and any innocent children, about to use the shortcut, would be interrogated. On my daily foray to the shops for my mother I would avoid eye contact with the policeman standing like a sentry at the side of the van. I would walk passed staring down at the pavement waiting with dread for a voice. "Oi, you!"

Some years later with the notorious railway fire, along with the station, consigned to history and a police crime file marked 'unsolved', Willie built a rocket.

Memory Spill

Influenced by the famous schematic centre page drawings in the Eagle comic and recent news of Russian dogs and monkeys being sent into orbit, Willie had decided that he would design and build his very own rocket. A large one. Essential to the launch was a propellant: a lot of it. Persuaded by his enthusiasm our gang agreed to donate the gunpowder from our fireworks as fuel for his projectile.

This was a big ask. We revelled in our seasonal activities which involved harassing the town's population by lobbing penny bangers, our weapon of choice, at innocent bystanders, creating shock and awe. More shock than awe. We roamed around like small suicide bombers with our pockets crammed with explosives, enough, if things went wrong, to blow a leg off at the thigh.

Willie constructed the rocket with his proud father looking on in admiration and offering encouraging comments. It was large tubular object with a pointy nose cone, fins and supported on four spindly legs. Based on my avid reading of comics featuring daring stories of the Second World War I saw a bomb; our father, impressed by his eldest son's scientific endeavours, a Starship. If the house insurance company had known NASA had set up a branch office in Bonnyrigg, dad's policy would have been cancelled. Suspicious that he might have gone beyond the realms of reality, I kept a close eye on my hamster Tag. I could imagine the headlines in the Dalkeith Advertiser: First Hamster in Outer Space.

Over the weeks leading up to Guy Fawkes Night, the body of Willie's rocket packed with gunpowder from our dismantled bangers and other fireworks and, I suspect, with other chemical substances. The previous Christmas, to my brother's manic glee, a chemistry set had been his main present; a reckless gift from our indulgent dad. Soon after, strange smells and noises had seeped from 'down the back' and odd events occurred. A hole of about two inches in diameter appeared in our garden bench, one of the church pews salvaged the demolished village church. The hole with scorched edges penetrated clean through the inch-thick seat panel. My mother and father looked at the hole, scratched their heads and talked in hushed voices, of Acts of God and meteor particles from outer space. But I knew; not how, but who.

Launch day arrived and on a clear moonlight night Willie's rocket stood on a plywood board, placed there at my father's insistence to protect the lawn. The centrepiece of the year's display pointed menacingly at the stars.

The evening kicked off with a paltry show of the fireworks bought by my dad from some dodgy shop on Leith Walk close to his office. Limp Roman candles spluttered, and one firework called Vesuvius, spewed some molten substance down its sloping side. The display reached its finale as a large Catherine Wheel spurted an angry jet of flame but failed to turn. It was time for the main event.

Willie advanced across lawn and lit the slow burning fuse, a product of his chemistry experiments, and retreated. Under a cloud of frosty bated breath, we watched as Willie counted down the seconds to take off. 10, 9, 8, 7, 6, 5……..

Before he reached four the rocket burst into life. With more fizz than a roar it jigged about like a demented Riverdance performer then, failing to defy gravity, fell over to lie facing our small family group and hissed threateningly.

Memory Spill

Drawing on his wartime experience as a Master Gunner in the Royal Artillery, he now saw a bomb not a rocket. Shocked into action he shepherded us down the garden path away from the potential blast zone.

There was no explosion. The rocket, in its death throes roared into life and sped around the lawn in ever increasing circles before expiring in the rose bed. Our father, his hand on his eldest son's shoulder, commiserated with the young von Braun unaware of the intricate Celtic pattern scorched in the lawn which would only be revealed at sunrise.

The Starship failure didn't dent Willie's fascination with rocketry and explosives. The following year he experimented with fuses that burned at different speeds. 'Down the Back' was festooned with pieces of string hung from a clothes line that spanned the room. Willie had dipped lengths of string in some chemical from his chemistry set, probably salt peter. Like some mad boffin, he would light pieces of differing length and time the rate of burn. Dad would stand and watch Willie at his experiments and discussed the results with him, a keen professor chatting with an unhinged student. I would stand to one side thinking one result could be our home burning to the ground. Crucially dad failed to ask the vital question: what was the purpose of producing slow burning fuses?

Unknown to my dad Willie had been constructing a miniature Peenemünde rocket site in the shelter of the broad rhubarb leaves. He had converted the obsolete sandpit into a missile silo. The pit now had a lid which when lifted revealed a launching ramp with spaces for half a dozen rockets. When armed, the ramp had a capacity for half a dozen rockets with bangers attached with Sellotape. The rockets and bangers were all fitted with Willie's slow burning fuses and aimed at our arch enemy of the moment, the owner of the chicken farm over the wall from our patchwork of back gardens. I've no

Memory Spill

recollection why we had fallen out with the chicken farmer, but we tended to have occasional disputes with adults in the neighbourhood. Whatever it was, Adolf Hitler would have been impressed with Willie von Braun's contribution to the war effort on the Bonnyrigg front.

On the launch night, under a full moon my brother slipped out of the house and crept down the garden and lit his home-made fuses, each timed to set a rocket off at half hour intervals. At midnight, the first rocket would roar into the air to deliver its explosive payload into the farmer's yard. As we were in bed, we could only imagine the annoyed chicken farmer, woken by the banger explosion and his chicken's frantic squawking, looking out of his bedroom window. As the second rocket arrived at 12.30 and its banger went off, he would be out in his yard in his dressing gown. By the time the sixth rocket landed he would be out of his mind. In the morning, Willie, would sneak down the garden and close the lid on his secret launch apparatus.

After an interval of a few days a second night attack took place, but this time as Willie left the house in the morning to close the lid on his launcher he spotted the haggard chicken farmer standing in his yard in deep conversation with Sergeant Turner. It was time to decommission and dismantle the launch site.

Today, my brother is a law-abiding citizen and to my knowledge has never in his adult life committed arson. Although, when he has ever been in charge of a barbeque, I have always read the labels on my clothes to make sure that the fabric is fire retardant. Just in case I get too close.

Chapter 8
House of God

Every Sunday I would be scrubbed, hair brushed and dressed in my 'Sunday Best' to walk with my family, down the Wee Brae to the village church. In those days Lasswade Parish Church was the hub of our lives; but not in a reverent or religious way. The church was central to the social life of the village. Almost every communal activity involved members of the congregation; the Scouts, Guides, Brownies and Cubs, the social gatherings, dances, concerts and the Summer Fair. After the War my mum and dad had married in the church. Dad was a church elder and the treasurer and mum helped run the Brownies; Tawny Owl or Brown Owl or some such thing. Willie, my older brother and I were Cubs and Scouts.

Memory Spill

We children were present for the first half hour of the Sunday service to sing a psalm or a hymn and pray. My family occupied a pew to the right-hand side of the church, sometimes bathed in the kaleidoscope of colours, as the sun penetrated the tall stain glass windows. Between the windows stood the pulpit from where the minister would look down on his flock. In more God-fearing times he would have looked across at parishioners sitting in the balcony that swept around the back and sides of the church. The interior design of the Parish Church had a simple ambience but not austere; there was a warm and friendly atmosphere with colourful flower arrangements every Sunday with festive decorations at Christmas, and at Harvest Thanksgiving a small mountain of fruit, vegetables other foodstuffs grew around the base of the pulpit go for distribution to the pensioners and the needy in the parish.

In the pew in front of us sat Harry Fisher, a deaf parishioner of indeterminate age. As the congregation ended a hymn and sat back down in their unwelcoming hard pews, old Harry would still be bellowing the last line. His fellow parishioners, the choir and the minister, the Reverend Hutchinson would wait with Christian patience while his loud voice echoed and vibrated around the church interior as he took his seat. My mother with less patience, would stare up at the ceiling and we children would, sometimes without success, stifle a snigger.

The Minister delivered a brief, child orientated homily that often flew, like angels, far over our heads then we would be shepherded from the church and taken up the Wee Brae to the church hall where Sunday School was held. There, we would learn the books of the Bible and how to be good children. We would listen and reflect upon how we had failed to be good during the previous week. Sometimes our misdeeds would be insignificant: throwing a firework into a bus queue or pretending to place a coin in the collection plate while palming it intending to buy sweeties later. Other deeds, like burning the local railway station to the ground were more difficult to reflect on. We would listen to the Christian teachings while thinking how we would much rather be somewhere else.

After Sunday School we would walk down to the church entrance clutching our attendance cards; folded cardboard cards stamped with blue ink stars; a full complement of stars earning the holder a certificate issued on prize giving day. The adults would stand on the church steps gossiping while we children would scamper around, feral after being confined.

Then parents would speak in commanding tones to restore order and the parishioners would drift away to enjoy the day of rest. If the weather was pleasant, we would set out for a walk. From the church, we would cross Polton Road and descend the steps set between my Grandfather's long disused decorator's business workshop and the Post Office, cross the bridge that spanned the River Esk, inhale the toxic fumes, before climbing up the School Brae. Opposite the school, on the other side of the Brae, we followed a steep path that rose by the side of the bleak graveyard serenaded by the harsh call of the rooks in the tall trees.

The path levelled off and there was a stretch, buttressed by a brick wall built to prevent the path collapsing and sliding down the slope into the Clark's smallholding below. From there we had a panoramic view of the village, of the paper mill and the tall chimney on the left, then to the right the railway viaduct. My dad would point out buildings, the mill curling pond, things of interest, who built them and why. Then, to my mother's consternation I would walk, a tightrope walker, arms stretched out, along the flat top of the buttress wall, low on the path side but with a sheer drop on the other. Dad would walk close alongside, to catch me if I fell, "Och, don't fuss, Nell, he'll not fall." My mother tutted, unconvinced.

Memory Spill

We would meander along the Brae Head paths, passing large houses standing in bushy gardens bordered by high stone walls. We walked shaded by tall leafy trees. Sometimes we would pass our concealed gang huts and dens, obsolete or current; part of the secret lives of us children. On a hot day the air would be heavy with the smell of honeysuckle hung over walls and the pungent aroma of the garlic plants carpeting the ground between the trees. Garlic plants that Auntie Jen had once told me had arrived in Britain along with the Roman legionnaires who had built a fort, not far away, near Dalkeith.

On some occasions we would bump into residents of the large houses, sometimes householders who had been victims of our misdemeanours; a firework thrown over a wall, apple stealing or broken greenhouse glass. On one walk dad greeted someone he knew through the church; a man with a military bearing and a ruddy face. He responded to dad's greeting, then looked down at us.

He had last looked down at us only two weeks before. We had been playing in a small field of cereal: wheat or barley. The game involved crawling around the field; hide and seek on our knees. By the time the owner stopped us the field resembled an intricate maze. He was incandescent with rage. As we stood cowering his face turned puce and a hurricane of spittle flew over our heads; he would report us to the police, inform the school, tell our parents.........

Well, now he was standing in front of our parents. We shifted under his scrutiny. But he couldn't place us, couldn't reconcile the spotless children dressed in neat school uniforms with the filthy, vulgar urchins who had destroyed his crop; he just wasn't sure. As we walked off up the path behind our parents, I felt the strong sensation of a pair of eyes boring into my back.

Memory Spill

At one intersection, there was a tree occupied by a bee colony. It had been there forever, according to my mother; we believed her, she had spent her childhood in Lasswade too. Sometimes, our route would take us past Sir Walter Scott's house with its hatched roof and the cottage reputed to have been where Burke and Hare, the grave robbers lived. Or we would follow the path that dropped into the valley, and if we walked far enough, we would arrive at the ghostly ruins of a paper mill destroyed by a fire, now overwhelmed by ivy. Then, we would head home along the railway line, my brother Willie and I competing to see how far we could walk along the rusty steel rails before losing our balance.

Sleeper jumping, and rail balancing would stop as we reached the viaduct that carried the railway over the river. We would look through the railings and drop stones into the river far below. In winter, we would sometimes watch miniature figures slide curling stones across the ice of the pond in the paper mill owner's garden while other players wielded brushes to control the momentum of the stones. One hot summer day, we were spectators from our high vantage point, as a circle of men engaged in gambling, then an illegal activity, disperse in a panic as a policeman appeared striding down the grassy fields towards them from Polton Road.

We would arrive home, eager to shed our 'Sunday Best' clothes. In the summer, while the Sunday dinner was being prepared I would run around to the small shop, a wooden hut that stood in Eldindean Road, to buy a block of ice cream and a tin of Creamola Foam, a powder that when mixed with water made a wonderfully refreshing drink. The lady shop owner knew me as the brother of one of her loyal customers.

I would often stand beside Willie and watch as she reached under the counter and produced a packet of ten Woodbines. A single cigarette would be removed from the packet and passed to my ten-year-old brother as he slid two pennies across the worn surface of the counter. When funds were available whole packets of Woodbines or Capstan would pass across the counter top or even exotic brands; Gold Flake, Passing Clouds and Chesterfields. I spent my childhood sat in gang huts or woods in an acrid fog of fag smoke as Willie and his friends puffed away.

At various times during the year social events organised by the church would convene in the hall at the foot of the School Brae. This hall had a stage where local amateur thespians would perform to audiences sat on rows of green tubular steel and canvas chairs. For dances, the chairs would line the edge of the hall with surplus chairs stacked in a side room. Then, the parishioners would try to waltz over the knotty floor boards sprinkled with chalk powder to smooth their passage, or they would pound them with exuberance as they performed Highland Reels.

One evening sitting with some friends, waiting for the pieces and jelly and ice cream we watched an elimination dance. The adults would waltz past, then the Master of Ceremonies would lift the stylus from the spinning record to announce the elimination criteria.

"Any gentlemen wearing brown shoes please leave the floor."

Two contestants would walk away from the stationary dancers as the MC lowered the stylus was lowered back onto the spinning disc and the dancers swirled around the floor until the music and the dancers again stopped.

"Would the ladies wearing bracelets leave the floor," announced the MC. A gentleman would escort his partner to the seats.

In this way the dancers were culled, and as the dance floor emptied the announcements would become slightly risqué.

"Gentlemen wearing blue underwear please leave the dance floor."

Memory Spill

A couple looked at each other torn between Christian honesty and embarrassment at revealing the intimate details of the husband's underpants. Slightly flushed they sat down next to us.

At the end of the elimination dance the next record spun on the turntable. Kenny nudged me and nodded towards the large lady, wearing an apron, ploughing her way through the throng like an icebreaker. At nine years old I was the tallest of my peers and thus her partner of choice.

"Och, son, I'll take you for a birle roond the floor," she said. "I need a wee break from the kitchen."

I stood up and allowed myself to be led onto the dance floor. She clasped me to her, arranged my hands, then with surprisingly agility I was being propelled around the dance floor. It was like dancing with a polar bear dressed in an apron. My head was gripped between her large bosoms where the scent of lavender mingled with the smell of baking; a pleasant homely aroma. As we circumnavigated the dance floor, my new dance partner hummed to herself. She may have been a widow imagining she was dancing with her late husband or a spinster reliving some fading memory of romantic dalliance with a boyfriend. But, wherever she was, I was becoming disoriented. I heard the music stop and a muffled announcement that the next dance would be 'Strip the Willow', a ceilidh dance; my sort of dance. My partner released me; she to return to her sandwich making, me to walk back to my sniggering friends.

In the summer the local park was the venue for a host of events organised by the Church and the Scouts, Cubs, Guides and Brownies: The Summer Fair, fancy dress football matches and the Scout sports days. On one occasion the Summer Fair was organised with greater enthusiasm than usual. Mr Stewart, the PE teacher at the secondary school who was the driving force behind such events handed responsibility to the Youth Fellowship. To meet the challenge a committee was formed. Plans were made, and tasks delegated. Banners advertising the fair were slung between lampposts on the Main Street. This was quite a dangerous task; one evening my brother, on top of an extending ladder, was hoisting a banner up between the lamp standards a truck appeared around the corner. We just had time to shout up to Willie to let go of the banner before the truck swept it away draped across its windscreen.

Previous fairs had been a bit of a flop with low attendances. Something was needed, something special to draw the crowds. At one of the planning meetings someone had a bright and audacious idea; a minor television celebrity would be stalked in Edinburgh by a team of eager members of the Youth Fellowship and persuaded to open that year's Fair. To everyone's surprise the compliant celebrity agreed to forgo his Saturday afternoon golf to open our fair. At the next meeting someone mentioned that their father knew a vintage car enthusiast and he would bring his convertible car to the fair. It was the ideal vehicle to transport our guest from the village to the park.

On the day of the fair and in glorious sunshine the vintage car, glorious in its polished coachwork and glistening brass bounced down the potholed track to the park. The tanned luminary bounced about on the tanned leather of the back seat and waved as the car pulled up to the enthusiastic cheers of the crowd. The slightly disoriented celebrity stepped unsteadily out of the car and mounted the podium under the fluttering bunting. He stood looking around, gathering his breath, and his wits, wondering why he had agreed to offer his services as he noticed the stench of the river that was now overwhelming his aftershave. Coughing to clear his throat of the polluted air he ran his fingers through his dishevelled hair before giving a rousing speech then declared the Summer Fair open. Some of the crowd hung around to get an autograph, but most headed towards the stalls set out around the park looking for a bargain. The fair was a huge success. The planning and execution had been brilliant. Persuading the celebrity to open the fair was a masterstroke. In the same way that a sequel fails to match a fantastic film there was never another Summer Fair like it.

After attending Lasswade Parish Church Sunday School, the next stage in the church's religious education programme was Bible Class; then in my teenage years I joined the Youth Fellowship. During a meeting, on a dark, driech, winters night we stepped over onto the dark side.

The Youth Fellowship met one evening each week and discussed topical stuff, with a Christian twist. There was plenty to discuss, it was the mid-60s; war was raging in Vietnam, Civil Rights demonstrations were on TV, Kennedy had been assassinated, Space, the final frontier was being conquered and the Cold War, with the ever-present threat of nuclear was annihilation, was in full swing. A local person of note would sometimes offer to give a talk. But, for teenagers there was now more pressing matters: Pop Music, fashion trends and television. The attendance at the meetings, like the Scouts, became sporadic. One dark, wet November night there was a gathering of only five members in the cold church hall. I have no recollection of who was there but there was at least one girl, the rest boys.

As the large bunch of keys, collected from the Beadle to unlock the hall, included the keys to the church we decided to use the vestry for our meeting. This was a small room, off the church, where the Minister changed into his robes before a service, wedding or funeral. The vestry would be much cosier than the cold and draughty Hall. We locked up the hall and braving the wind and drizzle, we sloped off down the path, illuminated for brief moments by the moon, through the church garden and settled ourselves round the meeting table in the vestry.

Memory Spill

On this evening, there was no enthusiasm for putting the world to rights. Bored, we chatted about the latest singles chart, examined the Reverend Kennedy's garments and tasted a little from a bottle of wine, unfermented for the sober Scottish Protestant communion. What to do?

I, along with my brother and friends, had dabbled with a Ouija Board. On our kitchen table, we had contacted amongst others, a dead miner and a distant relative, although there was always the lingering suspicion that someone was manipulating the glass, pushing it around the letters and numbers for a laugh. My fellow members of the Youth Fellowship listened to my description of all this and how anyone could set up a Ouija Board. As we were sitting around a circular table, it was all too tempting.

A brief rummage in a desk drawer produced a felt tip pen and a pad of paper. Soon the alphabet and numbers, a Yes and No, were written on squares of paper, and arranged around the table. A candle was lit and four fingers placed on top of an upturned glass. To avoid cheating we delegated the fifth person to take down the message we would receive and watch the possessors of each of the four digits to make sure they didn't look at the glass. The imprudence of performing a séance in the Parish Church, a place of God, was not considered; in our excitement and curiosity; we were about to dance with the devil.

"Is anyone there?" the observer in a quivering voice.

Memory Spill

Nervous fingers twitched, and the glass moved. We held our collective breaths; the candle guttered.

"Is anyone there?"

The tumbler moved again; with a squeak it slid over the oak table top to the paper square with 'Yes' written in capital letters. In unison four suspicious pairs of eyes looked up, then back down at our feet.

"Are you a man?"

Squeak, squeak, the tumbler arrived at 'Yes'.

"Who are you?"

Nothing.

"Who are you?"

No answer.

"Ask what happened to him!" hissed one finger.

"What happened to you?" Our observer enquired.

At this point the tumbler slid, squeaking and scraping across the polished top, to one letter, then to the middle, then to another letter. It was spelling something out. The tension was palpable. Rain spattered against the window pane, the door rattled in the wind and a shaft of moonlight slid across the table top.

K, squeak, squeak, I, scrape, L, squeak, scrape, L, squeak, E, scrape, D.

"What's he saying?"

"Killed." The observer, with a tremulous voice. "He says he was killed!"

"Jings!"

At this point the glass skidded around, backwards and forwards: K.I.L.L.E.D, K.I.L.L.E.D, and K.I.L.L.E.D. Then it squeaked to a stop. At this point we should have stopped too. But we were inquisitive, we needed to know more.

Memory Spill

"How were you killed?"

Our Spirit visitor declined to answer. Our inquisitor tried another tack.

"Where were you killed?"

The glass, instantly set out across the table moving backwards and forwards.

Y, squeak, U, scrape, G, squeak, squeak, O, scrape, S, scrape, squeak, L, squeak, A, scrape, V, I, sqeeeeeeeek, A.

"Yugoslavia, honestly!" It sounded suspicious, far-fetched, "It spelt out Yugoslavia. Ah'm no kiddin'!"

Four pairs of eyes stared in disbelief at our observer.

"Ah'm really no jokin'." he confirmed.

"Okay, who are you?" demanded one of the 'fingers', speaking to the tumbler.

Squeak, squeak, squeak. The tumbler was on the move; we were about to receive an answer.

J.E.S.U........

"Christ!" our observer said under his breath.

The fingers were snatched from the glass, the light switched on and the candle extinguished. The evidence: the paper squares, the letters and numbers were swept up and pocketed. The Vestry door locked, we walked along the path to the Wee Brae, the actors in a horror movie. Tacit partners in an unmentionable event we said our goodbyes. My four companions headed down the brae to the well-lit main road, leaving me to the lonely climb up the Wee Brae to Bonnyrigg. The brae, lined with trees, creating a claustrophobic, dark tunnel. The wind whistled through the high branches and the Moon, through the scudding windswept clouds, illuminated ghostly forms. I was Tam o' Shanter, the subject of Robert Burn's poem, chased by imagined witches and ghosts. But unlike Tam, I was sober. Stone cold sober.

Memory Spill

The wind blew as 'twad blawn its last
The rattling showers rose on the blast
The speedy gleams the darkness swallow'd
Loud, deep, and lang the thunder bellow'd

That night, a child might understand
The Deil had business on his hand.

I arrived home, breathless, slightly dishevelled and disorientated, never so glad to be with my family. I don't think we, the participants ever talked about that night again. It all started as a bit of teenage fun, adolescent bravado, but, had we danced with the devil or had one of us been a brilliant joker?

Memory Spill

Chapter 9
Holidays We Had

My first memory of a holiday was sitting on a beach eating a jam piece seasoned with gritty sand that crunched in my mouth. I had a small yacht and the water it floated in was thick with jelly fish. My next memory is climbing through a gate into a cow pasture. I stood up then tripped and fell headlong into a pool of cow shit. The pasture was across the road from a cottage we were staying in somewhere along the coast of the Solway Firth. I was three years old.

During my childhood we had many happy holidays in the Solway Firth area. We would travel on various buses from Edinburgh taking a whole day to reach our destination: Gatehouse of Fleet. My dad must have pored over endless bus schedules and timetables planning the journey. Once there, we would stay in rented cottages, caravans or bed-and-

Memory Spill

breakfast places. Each day spent on the beach was an expedition. We packed bags with essential supplies - Towels, swimming costumes, a Primus stove, food and drink, buckets and spades. Then we would follow the road to the seaside to arrive when the tide was out.

On the beach we would walk past the salmon nets. If we were early enough, the fishermen might appear in an old American army Jeep with a white star painted on the bonnet. Sometimes we would leave our bags on the sand to watch the fishermen lift the wriggling fish from the pools of water and hit them on the head with a small wooden club called a priest. Walking on we would reach a small cove and set up camp. Within an hour the fast tide would slide down the estuary cutting off from civilisation for hours. We swam in water, warmed by the Gulf Stream and the heat from the sand of the estuary, climb rocks and explore the woods of the Cardoness Estate behind us. On the sand dad would mark out a tennis court and we would play tenniquoit, a game in which a rubber ring is thrown over a net. Happy times.

On other years, less memorably, we would holiday in the Highlands to enjoy a less temperate climate and stare out of the windows of holiday cottages or bed-and-breakfast bungalows at swathes of rain sweeping across dark loch and if it was sunny we would be eaten by swathes of midges.

Then, in 1962, before foreign holidays became the norm, we went on a mini tour of Europe. In his youth, our father had cycled around northern Europe with his brother Bill. He must have wanted his sons to have a similar experience. Sailing from Leith to Antwerp we travelled through Belgium, Luxembourg, Germany and Holland. On the day of departure, we followed dad along the pier and stopped to look up at the bow of a large ship. But dad had kept on walking. We picked up our rucksacks and followed him. Our ship, or boat was a small tramp steamer moored in the shadow of the much larger ship. We were sailing with eight other passengers and a cargo of heifers. I spent most of the voyage sat on the deck inhaling the salty air that had a hint of the smell of cow shit, thrilled to bits as the vessel bobbed up and down in the choppy sea. My mother, less thrilled spent most of her time in the cabin, sea sick. What the heifers made of it I dread to think. It was an amazing and exciting holiday because dad had booked nothing apart from the sea crossings. We travelled between towns on buses and trains with wooden slatted seats, buses turning up expecting to find vacancies at pensions or hotels on the route. We visited the Atomium in Brussels, noticed the still war damaged buildings in Germany, sailed up the Rhine and on the canals of Amsterdam and there enjoyed ice cream in the beautiful Vondelpark now better known as a place to enjoy a joint or snort a line. One sultry evening in Amsterdam our father led us into a restaurant where we waited for menus. We could hear muttering behind a curtained archway, then a shifty looking man with a thin moustache weaved between the tables and whispered in dad's ear. Dad's face turned a shade of pink that matched the linen table cloths, then he shepherded us out into the street escorted by the brothel manager.

The following evening as we left Amsterdam a huge electrical storm raged around us, and a force 8 gale buffeted the ship. Our mother soon forgot about the embarrassing brothel visit as the ship pitched and rolled alarmingly. When we arrived home in a taxi, our father had no money left to pay the driver and he had to borrow the fare from a neighbour who must have been disappointed that the Wilson boys had returned home. It had been a wonderful experience which influenced a later holiday. An Italian holiday.

A holiday in Italy had been floated in a bar in Edinburgh. Floated is an apt expression. There were at least five of us, all students, drinking copious pints of Heavy and Special beer in

Memory Spill

the Cambridge bar. Then, in the 1960s drinking time ended at 10 o'clock with a ten-minute period of grace to consume the drinks already on the table. Grace didn't quite describe the rush to the bar to get in yet another round of drinks; the space in front of the bar was like the penalty area in extra time of a football match. We then drank the drinks already on the table and then the fresh round of drinks before staggering out into Young Street. The intake of excessive alcohol combined with the sudden exposure to cold Scottish air resulted in us all being in Scottish parlance, 'miraculous'. Our excited discussion about the holiday continued in the Italian ambiance of the Capri restaurant in Leith Walk. This was one of our regular haunts. It had a great atmosphere, an Italian ambiance. Most of the clientele were, like us, miraculous. Toni, the proprietor, in a black suit with a bow tie and swept back silver hair had the air of a mafia godfather. We sat watching our pizza being prepared, dough spun in the smoky air by flapping hands then placed in the fiery wood fired oven, a process interrupted occasionally when the chef would vault the counter waving his pizza shovel as he barged through the door to pursue a diner leaving without paying. As we consumed pizzas, our holiday plan evolved. We would fly to Rome, look at the Colosseum and other ruins, then travel to Naples, visit Pompeii to see more ruins, and climb Vesuvius. As an experience it would have been miraculous, a miracle if we all went. As the months passed, the group number dwindled to two; my elder brother Willie and me.

Our father dropped us off at the Turnhouse Airport on the outskirts of Edinburgh, hugging us as if he never expected to see his sons again. He handed Willie a piece of paper with an address scrawled on it. My brother looked at it with a frown. "Take care of this, don't lose it," said our dad as though he had just headed over a segment of the Dead Sea Scrolls. "This is the address of a friend who lives near Naples. A place called Castel Volturno. If you're stuck, got any problems, he'll

Memory Spill

help you." We looked at our dad in mute curiosity. He had never mentioned that he had a friend near Naples. Soon after we were in the air on the first leg of our holiday.

We arrived at Heathrow and then travelled on to Rome in an Alitalia jet. In the days before mass foreign tourism the plane was empty. We felt like important businessmen or celebrities on a private jet. Landed at Fiumicino Airport late at night. So late it was nearly morning. It would have made sense to sleep on the seats in the airport and wait to catch a bus in the morning. But, we fell for the friendly taxi driver routine, the taxi driver who knows of an affordable hotel. Tired after the long journey we accepted the offer naively failing to ask how much the fare would be; which, unsurprisingly, was eye watering.

The drive from the airport ended in the centre of Rome going the wrong way up a one-way street. This illegal manoeuvre ended in a heated argument between our taxi driver and an irate fellow Italian, annoyed to find his way blocked. The archetypal Italian motorist, he stood protruding through the sunroof of his Cinquecento, the archetypal Italian car, his arms waving about and his voice waking everyone in the neighbourhood, some of whom hung out of their apartment windows, adding a backing chorus. Eventually a truce was declared, and the taxi mounted the pavement skirted the Cinquecento and pulled up outside the hotel. The unremarkable appearance of the entrance gave the taxi drivers promise of 'affordable' credence but the interior design of the bedroom looked luxuriously unaffordable. We had not realised that we had been dropped off at the rear entrance.

In the morning we woke, at least I did, as Willie was never an early riser, to the sounds of revving cars, car horns, rasping scooters and sunlight forcing its way around the edge of the expensive drapes. I pulled on the cords and the curtains slid open. Our room overlooked a large ornate fountain, the Trevi Fountain, famous from the film 'Three Coins in a

Memory Spill

Fountain'. We were enjoying the hospitality of the Hotel Sant'Angelo. Expensive hospitality. We would need all the coins in the fountain to cover the bill. I roused my brother, and we dressed and walked through the ornate reception under the suspicious scrutiny of the concierge concerned that we were doing a 'runner'. We stepped out into the searing sunlight, searing heat and stinking exhaust fumes, to look for the Italian equivalent of a greasy spoon.

After a continental breakfast we sought a more suitable, affordable hotel and returned to the Sant'Angelo, paid the eye watering bill for our one night's residence and carried our suitcases out, passing the sour faced concierge who had given up the expectation of a tip.

For a few days we settled into a routine; sleeping, eating and drinking, and sightseeing. We were impressed by the Colosseum, enchanted by the views over terracotta roofs washed by the light of the setting sun, sat with the hippies on the Spanish Steps, dodged the insane Italian drivers as we crossed roads and wandered through the Basilica di San Pietro: St Peters, Lilliputians awestruck by the scale and grandeur. At night we sat outside restaurants and cafes in the warm evenings we dined on pasta and pizzas washed down with cold lager. The Romans were friendly enough. One evening a particularly friendly Roman sat down at our table introducing himself as Chico.

It's funny how, friendless in a large alien city, you overlook the swarthy, rodent features of a new companion. We ignored, at our peril, the furtive, feral eyes beneath the rim of the stained leather trilby hat. And being naively open to friendship our judgement was blunted by the state of near lager induced miraculousness. For an hour we enjoyed Chico's broken English banter before he suggested we go to his club, an exclusive one, of which he was a member. That Chico would be a member of an exclusive club was ludicrous; another warning sign that flew over far above our heads.

Memory Spill

We followed our new friend who was navigating through a piazza thronged with strolling family groups: mothers, fathers, children and funereal grandmothers. We pivoted left up a dimly lit cobbled side street and arrived at what appeared to be a corner cafe undergoing an interior refurbishment, the insides of the windows covered with newspapers. Steps led up to an entrance door with a rectangle cut in the newspapers, a viewing aperture. Chico rapped on the glass. After a few moments a pair of eyes appeared framed by the slot followed by a rapid exchange in Italian. There was a series of clicks as the door was unlocked and opened by a man, a doppelgänger of Toni, our friend, the maître d' of the Capri restaurant in Edinburgh; now a world away. Ushered through the door into the mysterious café, we passed through a portal into another world. There was a faint smell of cakes, a counter on one side and shadowy figures sat at tables. In the far corner an orange glow emitted from a stairway.

Chico gestured to us to follow, and he disappeared down the stair. Then vanished altogether. At the bottom of the stairs we found ourselves in a large cellar. It was older than the modern retail unit above, with a vaulted brick ceiling, stone floors and sumptuous sofas upholstered in cream upholstery, that stood on, appropriately as things turned out, shag pile rugs. Large table lamps, standing on glass and chrome side tables, cast a warm subtle light over what, as an interior design student, I could see was a stunning modern Italian interior. We sat down, sank into one sofa and looked around the stunning modern Italian interior then looked sideways at each other.

Our admiration of the room ended with the appearance of a group of women who sashayed through an archway, one bearing a bottle of champagne and glasses on a tray. The cork popped, and drink flowed into glasses as the scantily dressed creatures arranged themselves around us. They were the

Memory Spill

most beautiful, alluring women we had ever seen. We were intoxicated, not only by the champagne or the heady cloud of perfume, but by the interest the bevy of beautiful women were showing in us as they chatted in exotically accented English.

"You are Amerrikan, no?" Enquired the lady sat next to me as her slender hand tiptoed across my thigh on a long red talon tipped fingers that stabbed through the fabric of my chinos. I looked down at her hand in alarm.

"No, I'm Scottish, from Scotland." I muttered.

"Skot-land, mmm." My companion, mulled over the name of my homeland, "Skot-land, where is Skot-land?"

I enlightened her. "It's a part of Great Britain, above England."

"So, not from Amerika?" "No."

The finger tips hesitated, ceased their slow march across my thigh. "Mmmm......." She considered this; a diner in a restaurant, expecting a spicy taste but finding the soup bland. "....... Yes, I think I hear of Scozia."

I didn't think she meant that she had heard the rumour that the Scots had invented almost everything on Earth. More probably she had heard the that the Scots had invented the word 'parsimonious'. I was not one of the American youths, sons of millionaires that loitered at the bottom of the Spanish Steps affecting to be Hippies, with allowances the size of the NASA budget. Her disappointment was tangible. It took a while, at least three cork pops before I realized we were sitting in a brothel. We were way out of our depth. We needed to leave.

Ignoring the wandering fingers stabbing through my trousers I half turned to look at my brother. A hand had slipped into his cheesecloth shirt and was rummaging about like a hamster building its nest; older and wiser than me, it was hard to tell if he was enjoying the experience. For a moment a memory washed over me. The unintended visit to the brothel in Amsterdam which my dad thought was a restaurant.

Unlike our dad in the Amsterdam we didn't need to be told what we were in. But it wasn't just a brothel we were in, we were in trouble. Big trouble. Disentangling ourselves, we muttered our excuses and headed for the stairs leaving the prostitutes milling about, predatory insects watching their prey escape. But escaping the clutches of the Ladies of the Night was one thing, getting past the Mafiosi minders upstairs was another.

"Un momento, per favore." It was our doorman, now standing behind the café counter. We looked around feigning puzzlement as though we thought he was speaking to someone else while Willie reached for the door handle to open the door. It was locked.

"There is the small matter of the champagne, signors," said the man behind the bar in accented English, laced with menace. "Quattro bottiglias, signors."

We protested. We couldn't have consumed four magnums of champagne. But four corks had popped, and the bill had to be settled. Would be settled. Two shadowy figures sat at the table behind us stood up, chairs scraping over the tiled floor, to stand close behind us. Very close. This tacit threat, accompanied by a warm garlic laced breath persuaded us to produce our now woefully thin book of traveller's cheques. With trembling hands, we signed away another small fortune. With the cheques scrutinised, the thug behind the bar nodded to one of his associate thugs who, with calculated politeness, opened the door and ushered us out.

As we stood on the pavement, stunned by the evenings events, the door swung open and Chico stumbled down the steps and landed in an undignified pile at our feet. As we stared down at our erstwhile friend contemplating whether take him to the hospital or steal his wallet in compensation, the door opened, and his leather trilby spun through the air to land on his inert body.

Resisting the urge to kick our companion while he was down, we set off for the local police station to seek redress. We were ushered into a small interview room furnished with a desk, two chairs, and as it was two o'clock in the morning, a polite and attentive policeman.

The telling of our tale of woe produced sympathetic shakings of the head followed by theatrical shoulder shrugs. As we left the room the policeman pointed at our feet, sketching the shape of a shoe box. "Count yourselves lucky," he said, "you could be at the bottom of the Tiber wearing.... what do you English say? Concreta shoes." His mirthless laugh followed us down the corridor. But luck was what we needed now. Three days into our Italian adventure all we had left were a few traveller's cheques, the return plane tickets and a scrap of paper with the address of a friend of our dads who, our dad assured us, would help us if we were stranded. The friend lived in Castel Volturno, near to Naples. Then, in the 1960s a long way from Rome.

The next morning, nursing stupendous hangovers, we were sitting having a continental breakfast in the 'greasy spoon' café. On the table top we had laid out the two thin travellers cheques books, a few lira bank notes, and a crumpled piece of paper with our dad's mystery friend's address written on it: a street in a town called Castel Volturno near the city of Naples. We were having a session of 'blue sky' thinking; how to get to Castel Volturno. Train, bus, hitchhike?

As we pondered our predicament, we noticed a sign tied to the lamppost next to our table. It advertised scooters for hire for a price that didn't look like a mortgage repayment. We finished our meagre meal and, suspecting that the scooter hire deal was too good to be true, set off to find out. It was the turning point in our Italian adventure. The people renting the scooters seemed genuine, and the deal equally so.

As the manager filled the rental forms with our details we smiled and mentioned a bit of local sightseeing in Rome as the purpose of hiring the Vespa. Considering the lunatic Roman drivers, a 'bit of sightseeing' in Rome was probably riskier than the journey to Naples which we had in mind. When, with his pen hovering over the insurance section he asked about the history of accidents, we kept schtum about Willie coming off his motorbike on the wet cobbles of Bonnyrigg High Street and sliding under Father Gallagher's Ford Anglia. His helmet probably saved him serious injury then, but we would have no such protection if we fell off this scooter. Within half an hour we rode out into the mayhem of Rome's roads and weaved our way to our hotel to pack and settle the bill.

Later that morning we took the bulk of our clothing and possessions, crammed into one suitcase, to the left luggage facility in the nearest railway station, the Roma Termini. A serious official in intimidating martial uniform had asked us to open the bulging suitcase probably thinking it might contain a body. He then thrust a long rod into the case, some sort of electronic sniffer, to check for Semtex. We weren't surprised he was po-faced. This was the era of the Baader Meinhof and the Brigate Rosse left wing terrorist groups. Having dumped our excess baggage, we plunged into the chaotic traffic with the basic essentials strapped to the rack on the back of the Vespa scooter. With Willie at the handlebars and me balanced on the minuscule pillion seat we headed for Naples. We found the direction signs for Naples after twice circumnavigating a large, endless, roundabout; a Ben-Hur moment; the race scene but with cars instead of chariots.

For the first stage of the journey we travelled on a motorway, probably illegally, burbling along the hard shoulder until we left on a slip road to drive across a line of jagged

Memory Spill

mountains before descending to the coast. As we rasped along I would watch, over my brother's shoulder, as beetles of various sizes flew across our path. Willie's head would twitch, and the scooter would wobble when a larger bug would strike his face like the impact of a meteor on a planet. On the snaking mountain road trucks roared passed us within touching distance on one side as we looked down a steep rock strewn, pine clad slopes on the other. At one point a red Ducati motorbike roared passed, the rider, dressed in red and black, leaning over with élan as he cornered at speed. Later we passed the same motorbike lying inert, on its side. Nearby a scrum of people crowded around the front of a large articulated truck as a man looked under at the body of the motorcyclist who had, with such élan, passed us. Sobered by the accident that had befallen our fellow biker we travelled on with a little more care. We rested, sat in roadside cafes eating squares of pizza in the cool mountain air and in a haze of diesel fumes. We followed the snaking road until we caught sight of the coast and the sparkling sea in the distance. We entered Castel Volturno as the sun was setting.

We entered a piazza that seemed to be the centre of the town. There was an abrupt silence as Willie turned off the rasping engine. My brother lit a cigarette, and we stood in the warm evening air looking around as the cooling engine made small metallic ticking sounds that competed with the ever-present noise of cicadas. On one side of the square light spilled from a bar, empty, apart from a barman with a thick moustache polishing glasses behind a counter. The only sign of life. "Buona sera, Come stai?" Said the man as we entered, a tooth pick moving up and down like a miniature conductor's baton under the moustache.

"Buona sera...... do you speak English?" Willie asked optimistically.

"Sì, a little."

Memory Spill

"Do you have a room... eh... a stanza?"

"I regret, no." Our faces fell. This was bad news.

"But I think I may help you," he said, a line of nicotine stained teeth still gripping the toothpick appeared beneath the moustache. "Mi chiamo Federico. Follow please."

I glanced sideways at my brother, apart from his aviator sunglasses his face spattered with the corpses of flying insects. Was this a kidnapping attempt, did Federico think we were members of a wealthy family? Was he a member of the local Mafia? A few years later Italian mobsters would kidnap John Paul Getty III. They cut off his ear and sent it to his obscenely wealthy, but disinterested dad. Our dad was a banker but not in the obscenely wealthy range.

Willie shrugged his shoulders: we had run out of options. We waited on the pavement while Federico locked up the bar, then follow our new amico around the corner. We were more than apprehensive; our last 'amico' had enticed us, into a Roman brothel, with disastrous results. But Federico, the friendly barman wasn't leading us into a trap. He had no intention of kidnapping us and sending ransom demands to our family in Scotland. We followed him through a gap in a hoarding, then through a gold framed smoked glass door into what was a hotel reception, a vision in honey coloured marble.

"Is new built," said Federico, stating the obvious, "I take care."

"Caretaker?" asked Willie, clarifying Federico's position.

"Si, si," Federico grinned in the gloom. "Follow."

We padded down a corridor behind our new amico. He stopped outside a door which he opened with a theatrical flourish.

"Entrare!"

Memory Spill

The bedroom had a chandelier hanging from the centre of the ceiling over two single beds draped with dust covers. Other pieces of furniture, a dressing table, wardrobe, chairs and a circular occasional table draped with dust covers resembled ghosts in the moonlight. Federico walked across the room and closed the full-length curtains, pulled the dust cover off a standard lamp and switched it on. A door in the corner led to an en-suite bathroom, the walls faced in a creamy marble with a bowl to wash your feet in. We were in a recently built hotel ready to open for business.

We were about to be the first guests. "You like, si," said Federico. Was he offering us the room? Then Willie asked the important, twenty million lira question.

"How much?" Then in case Federico didn't understand he rubbed his fingers together in the international sign language.

Federico shrugged and smiled. "Niente."

Nothing! Amazed we shook his hand and thanked him profusely.

Once Federico left we showered and lay, wrapped in the dust sheets, on the beds. "Jings, Willie. This is great!" There was no reply, just a gentle snoring. It had been an epic journey and my brother, the nocturnal one, had been the pilot. I had only been the passenger. In the morning we would look for dad's friend. We had breakfast in Federico's bar. We thanked him, and Willie gave him some of his tax-free cigarettes to show our appreciation of his kindness.

Federico gave a depreciating shrug of the shoulders. He smiled. "I am a father to two boys. But they are younger than you, si? I would like someone do the same for them. Maybe in your country, in England, eh?"

Overwhelmed we suppressed the urge to point out we were not English. We left the piazza with the rasp of the Vespa bouncing off the buildings and set off along the coast.

Memory Spill

Directions from Federico meant we knew where we were going. Our father's friend's villa stood somewhere on a small and exclusive estate that lay between the coast road and the vivid blue sea, a sprawl of white walls and terracotta tiled roofs.

This otherwise idyllic view was marred by a man of brick shit-house proportions, dressed in a quasi-military uniform holding a pump action shotgun. He wore aviator sun glasses with mirrored lenses. The type of sun glasses through which you can't see the wearer's eyes only a disconcerting reflection of yourself. We pulled into the entrance and stopped alongside the security guard. Arriving unannounced and uninvited, the guard was both a surprise and a problem.

"Si?"

"Il nostro padre amico Mr Hutchinson," explained Willie showing the piece of paper with the address in our father's spidery writing.

The guard grappling with Willie's phrase book Italian, scrutinised the note for a while; a Bletchley Park code breaker trying to decipher a message transmitted from Berlin to a U Boat hunting convoys in the North Sea.

"Passporte favoure."

He took our passports, peered at each photo and peered at us. I was relieved that we had showered that morning and the insect graveyard had been washed from Willie's face. Satisfied that we were not a cell of the Brigate Rosse terrorist group planning to cull the filthy capitalist villa owners he motioned for us to leave the Vespa and walk up the road in front of him; in front of his shotgun. We arrived at the villa with the guard on our heels with his shotgun slung under his arm. As we walked down the drive way, we realised that the villa stood on the edge of a golden beach and the shimmering blue Mediterranean Sea. For a moment I had

Memory Spill

a mental picture of us running down the golden beach and playfully throwing ourselves into the waves. Our armed escort had different thoughts altogether.

"Stand!" He commanded pointing with the barrel of his gun at a spot to the right of the doorway; just in case we had any thoughts about running down to the beach and playfully throwing ourselves into the waves.

He knocked on the door. We held our breath. Footsteps approached followed by a nervous questioning voice. The guard answered. The person on the other side of the door seemed satisfied and with a rattle of chains the door swung open. A petite, attractive woman stood in the doorway looking at the two of us with a faint smile and her eyebrows raised as the guard gave his report in Italian. Then Willie gave a rambling travelogue of our journey from Edinburgh and explained that our dad was a friend of her husband. Reassured that we were not terrorists intent on kidnapping her she thanked the security guard, introduced herself as Penny. She led us into the villa an asked us to make ourselves comfortable in the lounge then disappeared. As we sat on the cream fabric sofa looking out at the sea, we could hear a muffled voice somewhere depths of the villa; the lady of the house speaking on the telephone, breaking the surprise news to her husband.

The door opened, and Penny reappeared with a reassuring smile. "Okay, Andy will be home later this afternoon." she said." I'll sort out a room for you and give you some lunch."

Then, probably concluding that our state of uncleanliness was a threat to her expensive furnishings. "Why don't you go down to the beach for a swim?" Adding, "you'll have it all to yourselves. It's private."

And it was. The deserted pristine beach had a wire fence running from the estate down to the edge of the sea to

Memory Spill

keep the rabble at bay. The wind had piled up colourful food wrappers and newspaper pages, against the fence on the peasant's side stopping the private beach from being sullied by their litter. Willie and I ran down the golden beach and playfully threw ourselves into the waves then swam out and floated on the undulating sea. We looked back at the immaculate white villas and the cloudless blue sky above, savouring the moment. We dined 'alfresco' on the patio. To the gentle accompaniment of the lapping waves Penny told us about Naples, Pompeii, Vesuvius and other places of interest. Andy, she explained worked for Alfa Romeo, not the cars but the aerospace division. She was a lovely person. It was a relief to sit and talk with someone without the worry we would be robbed of our empty wallets.

In the evening Andy appeared. A short, stocky, fair haired Scotsman with lively eyes and an easy smile. Yes, he knew our dad. He was a client of dad's bank. We realized then that Andy was not an actual friend but a client who lived in the country where his sons would probably have needed rescuing from some disaster or other. He may have even given us the address without forewarning his client. I could imagine the phone conversation on the hissing line giving the news we had washed up in Castel Volturno.

"Mr Wilson, I have a Mr Hutchinson on the line. He'd like a word with you......he's calling from Italy...shall I put him through......" Our father, sat at his desk in the Granton branch of the Royal Bank of Scotland, would have looked out of his window at the grey sea of the Firth of Forth, gathering his thoughts while watching the seagulls soar and swoop under the grey cobbled sky. He would have sighed, with frustration but probably with relief. *"Yes, put him through please."*

Memory Spill

Back in Italy Andy explained to us we could stay a couple of days but then he and Penny had to return to the UK. Our faces fell. Andy laughed.

"Don't worry, I've sorted something out for you. I'll show you tomorrow," he said, "and in the evening, you'll meet our neighbours. We're all invited to a barbecue!"

The next morning after a continental breakfast Andy drove us to a holiday camp not far away from his villa. After a brief conversation with a man who appeared to be the caretaker we were shown to a room on the first floor of a block of holiday apartments that overlooked a large pool. The room was not as palatial as the bedrooms we had occupied on this holiday: the hotel in Rome or the friendly barista's hotel or Andy's villa but it was clean and serviceable. And it had a large swimming pool. Feeling obliged to show gratitude to the caretaker Willie gave him some of his dwindling supply of cigarettes; due to our dwindling supply of liras we could not pay any rent. Later I realised that during that telephone conversation between our father and his client payment for our accommodation in Naples would have been negotiated.

During the final days with Andy and Penny in their beach front villa we kept ourselves amused swimming in the warm sea or sunbathing on the beach under the envious gaze of the hoi poloi huddled together on the other side of the litter festooned fence. In the evenings we enjoyed barbecues with Andy and Penny's American neighbours. George and Mary were from somewhere in the American South. George was a large man with a big personality. A sort of John Wayne, not a 'red neck although he had a rather florid complexion. Mary, his wife was small, bird like and intense. They had an attractive daughter about fifteen and two younger sons.

The barbecue, the first of many, was a feast. Our only comparable experience was Scout camp bonfires with sausages on sticks and potatoes thrown in the embers while we sang 'Ging gang goolie'. This was a more sophisticated menu of thick steaks and fat beef burgers washed down with bottles of Budweiser beer. After the meal we had a strong black coffee laced with Sambuca, an aniseed flavoured liqueur. As homespun Scottish boys we all things American were fascinating and they, residents of the 'New World', wanted to learn about the 'Old country'. The conversations flowed to a background of Frank Sinatra songs. We soon discovered that George was a fan of 'Old blue eyes'.   In fact, he was so fanatical about Frank that he possessed every recording he ever released with collection displayed on shelves that ran the entire length of a wall of the lounge. His eldest son was, in that confusing American way, named George Junior and his younger son christened Frank in homage to his crooning hero. This generous American family would take care of us after the generous Andy and Penny left for the UK.

The next day, the day of our host's departure and our final day lounging about in their villa a violent storm swept the coast. Grey clouds scudded over a slate grey sea and crisp packets and newspaper pages blew free from the demarcation fence to join the gulls battling to keep their position in the gale. But the wind was warm; at least warmer than the seaside of the Firth of Forth. We decided, on this final day at the villa to have a swim regardless of the weather. Running down the beach through a thin salty mist we passed a group of astonished Italians dressed in thick coats and woolly scarves and launched ourselves into the rolling waves. We swam out some distance and turned to look back. The Italian beach walkers and the villa had disappeared. It was our turn to be astonished.

The wind has swept us down the beach; a long way down. Alarmed, I turned to look for Willie only to find he had disappeared too. Then, with relief I saw his head surface on the top of a rising wave some distance away then vanish. He was being dragged out to sea. I was near enough to swim for the shore where I reached a point where I could stand up. I staggered up the beach to find help. But help wasn't necessary. When I turned around Willie was standing Jesus like on the water. He had beached on a concealed sand spit. He was lucky. The next landfall would have been Sardinia.

Fifteen years later during a holiday in Wales I would regale a friend with this story, this tale of the near loss of my elder brother in a storm in Italy. It would lead to an extraordinary meeting on a windswept golf course in Abersoch. But in 1968 my brother survived, swam back to the shore where both of us trudged exhausted up the beach to the villa. Later that day we all gathered and watched Andy and Penny loaded their suitcases into his Fiat. "Don't you go worrying about these here boys," said George in his southern drawl, "we'll take real good care of them." We were about to experience the 'American Dream'.

With Andy and Penny gone we moved into the holiday camp which, on this second viewing, looked like a small Italian version of a derelict Butlins or a Hollywood set for in an apocalypse film. A far cry from the luxury of Andy's villa, it was beyond faded elegance. But, standing on the balcony we consoled ourselves with the fact it had a swimming pool and the knowledge that things could be a lot, lot worse. The resort had the air of a ghost town or an obsolete film set. As far as I could make out we were the only guests resort.

Every morning, before our self-catering continental breakfast we would carve our way through the flotsam of fly and beetle corpses and leaves that floated on the surface of the pool. It seemed that the duties of the caretaker didn't extend to taking care of the pool; or much else. When we weren't navigating through the pool debris, we filled our days with a visit to Naples where we had a run-in with the police when we drove up a one-way street in the wrong direction, a trip to Pompeii where we marvelled at the ruins and the

Memory Spill

petrified inhabitants and to a place where hot gasses hissed out of holes in the ground and the soles of our sandals felt as though they would melt.

At the holiday camp we would read or play chess on a minute travelling chess set; my brother the victor most of the time. And, we had permission to use the private beach to frolic in the sea without being shot by the security guard. Most evenings we were the guests of the Americans, enjoying lavish barbecues with Frank in the background singing 'My Way', his hit of that year. The Kinks, The Bonzo Dog Band, and the Beatles were my sort of music, but Ol' Blue Eyes grew on me.

"Have you guys ever been to a drive-in movie?" Asked George one evening while we sipped our Sambuca laced coffee. We explained that we while we were familiar with the term 'drive-in movie' it wasn't a common cinema experience in Scotland due to the inclement weather. Not for the first time during our short friendship the Americans looked at us with compassion as though their visitors were from a deprived country. The next night, with petite Mary at the wheel of their vast American automobile we all set off for the leisure centre on the US military base. It was the biggest car I had ever seen. My ex GPO Morris Minor van would have fitted in the boot, or as the Americans call it: 'the trunk'. We sat on the long leather front bench seat beside Mary as she manoeuvred the wallowing car down narrow rural roads, ghostly trees and hedges caught in the headlight beams rushed by. As I sat swaying in the middle of the front settee, I noticed the pedals had been built up with wooden blocks so that Mary's feet could reach them. When we arrived at the entrance to the military base, we stopped at a barrier where a sentry examined our passes while a torch beam flitted across our faces. Satisfied that we weren't terrorists or Russians the barrier swung upwards and we drove into the base through a tunnel.

The base was a sprawl of buildings enclosed in what appeared to be a vast extinct volcanic crater. In this area of

Memory Spill

Italy, it may have just been dormant, the magma bubbling beneath us. A dense pine forest clad the slopes that rose to the curved rim of the crater. Above, there was a backdrop of a star splattered black sky and the bright orb of a full moon. On the way through the base we passed between the playing fields set out for baseball and American football. Groups of footballers dressed like modern day gladiators caught in our headlights would trudge across the road in front of our car causing to Mary stab at her wooden block brake pedals. At least the sportsmen had helmets and armour-like kit to protect them if Mary couldn't reach the brakes.

Mary swung the car into the movie area. It was an enormous car park with a gigantic white painted concrete screen at one end. With our huge car parked amongst an armada of other huge cars we sat, windows open, and watched a forgettable movie in an unforgettable venue. To add to the surreal experience and to provide a pleasant distraction, a fire erupted amongst the trees on the hillside, flames leaping like solar flares into the night sky. Hyper with Coca Cola and stuffed with popcorn we drove back to our American friend's villa, said our farewells and headed off back to the holiday camp to pack ready to leave Naples. After a subdued and exhausting journey Back over the mountains we returned the scooter to the rental garage in Rome and caught the bus to the airport and the plane home. At Napier Technical College my classmates exchanged stories of their holidays. Jimmy, John and Dave had worked on the refuse collections and wore the retro clothes they had retrieved from the bins. Others recounted mundane holidays with their parents. I told my ripping yarn of our Italian adventure, only to be trumped by Maria who had got a job as an au pair in a in Sicilian town only to arrive during a ferocious gun fight between two Mafia gangs. Willie and I had brought back a bottle of Sambuca liqueur, but the combination Sambuca and black coffee didn't

106

impress our parents and to be honest, us. Some holiday experiences just don't travel well.

My story now moves forward a decade and a half to 1983. I had qualified as an Interior designer and moved from Scotland to the city of Leeds in England. I had married, fathered a daughter, gained a dog, and bought a caravan. It was a time when we went on summer holidays with friends, fellow caravaners. In the summer of that year we spent our holiday on a farm in Abersoch in North Wales. The weather was shocking. Ferocious squalls blew in from the Atlantic. The caravans pelted with rain rocked from side to side in the wind. One day we braved the weather and walked down to the beach with our respective dogs and watched the white capped waves sweep in to rush up the beach. The warm winds and the stormy scene brought memories flooding back. Memories of a holiday in Italy with my brother. As we sat on a rock, I told our friends the story. Of the colossal grandeur of St Peters, the visit to the Roman brothel, the scooter journey, the generous barista, my dad's 'friend', the American experience. And, of how the stormy beach scene in Wales had reminded me of how my brother had been swept out to sea.

It was part of our holiday routine that my friend Martin and I played golf. To avoid antagonising our wives we played first thing in the morning, as early as possible, and in any weather; rain or shine. The morning after my story telling session on the beach we set off from the first tee of Abersoch Golf Club in the teeth of a howling gale. Cocooned in plastic with bobble hats pulled down to our eyebrows we played along a fairway that ran parallel with beach. As we turned to play the back nine holes, we noticed a solitary golfer, also battling through the storm and catching us up. On the twelfth hole we waited at tee, and as demanded by golf etiquette we invited the lone golfer to play with us. He agreed, and after welcoming handshakes, we played on.

Memory Spill

"Do I know you? Have we met before?"

It was our new friend, his words swept away on the wind.

"I don't think so." I said. Under all the protective clothing and bobble hat, for all I knew, he could have been Jack Nicklaus.

"I do know you, you're Sandy. You and your brother Willie stayed with us in Naples, in our villa in Castel Volturno. I remember you fine."

It was the oddest encounter. Only the day after the telling of the event filled Italian adventure to my friends, Andy Hutchinson, the man who had been our salvation in Italy was standing before me.

Chapter 10
Ging Gang Goolie

Dress in my kilt, I Dib, Dib, Dibbed, gave the three-finger salute, and promised to obey the Queen. It was the evening of my initiation into the Scouts. I was eleven years old. I knew who the Queen was. She had walked past me in the park when she visited Bonnyrigg. We had walked from the school to line the entrance drive, wave small flags and cheer. The carpet factory had ceased production for the day; the smell of jute in the air was absent. Her majesty was fortunate that the royal progress did not include Lasswade. Closing the paper mill for a day would not clear the atmosphere. Even a week wouldn't have made much difference.

Our Scout troop had four patrols, each named after a bird. The Eagles, the Ospreys and the Kestrels sounded more glamorous than my patrol: The Owls. Inside the scout hall there was a canvas enclosure in each corner, one for each patrol. At the start of each session the patrols lined up and saluted while pledging allegiance to God and the Queen. The

Memory Spill

salutations to the monarch completed the Scoutmaster, Tommy Green would walk along the line. He would peer at the uniforms, admire the flat rim of the 'Canadian Mountie' hats (achieved by steaming and ironing) and here and there adjust a woggle before looking down at the polished shoes. If a silent fart escaped Tommy would look around with an expressionless face as we stifled childish sniggers. With the inspection over the Scoutmaster would follow the patrol leader into the patrol enclosure to run a critical eye over the interior.

Before the activities began we splashed water over the floor to subdue the dust. Then we would learn the scouting skills necessary for gaining the various badges; first aid, how to tie a Bowline knot with one hand; useful if you were holding on to an Alpine mountainside with the other, and how to make a stretcher out of scout staffs and two jackets. As seemed to be as many ways to fart as there was to tie a knot there should have been a badge for flatulence skills to wear proudly on our sleeves. When we weren't making stretchers, farting and building structures out of poles and string we played games. In the summer, we rambled through the local woods: the Braeheads following arrows and circles scratched into the paths or formed with twigs and stones by the scout leaders. As the dark winter months closed in we played indoor games.

One memorable game involved a boxing glove. The troop formed a circle facing inwards with eyes closed and hands clasped behind them. One of the scout leaders would walk around the circle carrying a boxing glove which he would place in the hands of one scout. Armed with the boxing glove the scout would then pummel his surprised and startled neighbour on the right with the glove as he chased him round the circle. Back in his place the victim would stand bruised and panting thinking what a bastard the pursuer was. The holder of the glove then placed the glove in the hands of another scout and the frantic pursuit began again; for some it was an opportunity to settle scores. Another, more cerebral game, involved finding an object for each of the letters of our name. Having a short name was helpful. One evening as we all milled around someone with the name Stuart arrived back. Amongst his hoard of objects was a small stone urn. The aghast Scout Master told the scout to return the urn to the graveyard as we all crossed ourselves.

I was still a cub when I first experienced the annual Scout camp trip. There were about four of us amongst the older boys dressed in their more grown up military attire. We gathered in a huddle outside the scout hall waiting for the bus that would transport us to the campsite.

A cattle wagon appeared around the bend and pulled in at the edge of the road, the driver peering at a piece of paper. He seemed lost and needed directions to a local farm. Tommy Green walked over and after a brief discussion and a lot of head nodding the driver jumped down out of his cab, walked to the back of the truck and dropped the ramp.

"Whits he dae'n, Sir there's nae sheep aboot here?" Said an anonymous voice from the back of the group.

"It's not for sheep," said Tommy. "This, son, is the bus."

"Fucking hell!" said the anonymous voice at the back in language that would have made Baden Powell blanch.

On church outings, we travelled on a single decker bus. If it was the Sunday School picnic, we would stand on the seats and unroll colourful streamers out of the high up small sliding windows and watch them flutter in the wind along with our shrieks and laughter. Then, on the way back we would sit or lie on the seats exhausted after sack races, egg and spoon races and rounders on the beach. This bus would have no seats or windows.

The released ramp fell to the ground with a clatter and we loaded the tents and cooking utensils then our baggage for the trip; rucksacks and army or navy kit bags that our fathers had brought home from the war stencilled with their names and numbers.

We assembled on the ramp of the truck for a photo shoot by our parents. We looked at the cameras and our mothers smiling trying to mask their anxiety and fathers grinning at the prospect of a week of peace. With the photo session over the scout leaders herded us like livestock into the back of the truck which reeked of recent occupants. A careless fart would have passed unnoticed in the stench. As the ramp clanged shut we stumbled about on top of the tents and kitbags looking for a comfortable place to sit. The engine burst into life sending a shudder and a cloud of diesel fumes though the truck. For a short while the fumes fought an uneven battle with the smell of cow shit, then as the truck picked up speed the fumes fled through the slats into the open air.

As we bounced and swayed along the country lanes we sat on our kit bags and tents, like paratroopers waiting to jump, and watched through the apertures as the green hedges rushed by. Then, as we slowed down to stop at a crossroad in a village a Scout mooed like a cow. A Cub then bleated like a sheep. Then we all joined in mimicking the cattle and sheep that would have been the normal cargo. The cacophony of 'moos' and 'baas' that came from behind the wooden slats startled the unsuspecting villagers. As they turned to stare the farm animal noises turned to raucous laughter.

Released from the cattle truck at the campsite we clattered down the ramp like a herd of beasts. The equipment was unloaded, tents set up in regimented rows and the latrine excavated; a long deep pit like a grave, with a canvas screen and as time passed an evil smell. There was a large tent that acted as a kitchen where, in the morning, you could watch the porridge cooking in an enormous black pot while one of the scout leaders tapped his fag ash into it.

Memory Spill

A flag pole marked the centre of the camp and each morning at daybreak before the day's activities began the Union Jack would be raised then unfurled in a ceremony that involved prayers, saluting and pledging allegiance to the Queen. Tommy Green and his assistants looking up at the flapping flag hoped it was the right way up. At sun down, we lowered the flag and folded it like a Japanese Origami paper folding ceremony and carried to the Scout Master's tent.

At the start of the day the tents we would tidy the tents ready for Tommy Green's inspecting of our kit and uniforms. The bed wetters would leave their sleeping bags out in the sun hoping that they would dry out before the next bedtime.

Once the inspections and inevitable chores were out of the way games occupied most of the day: rounders, hide and seek and kick the can. Or there were more serious scouting activities with each patrol competing to show their skills or lack of skills in the art of tracking or building things out of bits of wood and rope. On one night, there would be a midnight hike along the sand dunes and back through the woods. We would walk and stumble with the beams of torches arcing around like miniature air raid search lights. Tommy and his assistants would, with little success, try to subdue the ghostly wails as we tried to scare each other.

Most nights we sat around a camp fire holding mugs of drinking chocolate. As we watched the glowing sparks floating upwards to join the bright stars in the inky sky, we played parlour games or had a boisterous scouting singalong.

Ging gang goolie goolie goolie goolie watcha
Ging gang goo, ging gang goo
Ging gang goolie goolie goolie goolie watcha
Ging gang goo, ging gang goo
Hayla, oh hayla Shayla, hayla shayla, shayla, ooooh…..

Memory Spill

The livestock, trying to sleep in the neighbouring fields, must have been wondering what on earth was going on.

Later in the tents before lights out we would tell rude jokes, gruesome stories and sing gruesome songs:

'Have you ever seen a hearse go by and wondered what it was like to die, the worms go in, the worms come out, they go in thin and they come out stout, ha ha hee hee how happy we would be......'

After a few renditions silence would blanket the campsite as we drifted into a deep sleep surrounded by the hoots of hunting owls, the smell of damp grass, damp canvas and the whiff of the latrine.

At the end of the week the cattle truck came into view, swaying down the rutted track as though it might topple over and slide down onto the beach. We loaded the camp paraphernalia and our baggage and then we would stomp up the ramp jostling each other to find a comfortable spot. The return journey was much more subdued as we sat thinking of the home comforts waiting for us and of our parents; Mums and dads we now realised we had missed. Our parents too, rediscovered their love and fondness as they cuddled our unwashed reeking bodies when we disembarked back in Lasswade.

Bob a Job Week was one highlight of the Scouting calendar. Tommy Green, would hand out the record cards along with encouragement to do our best, our duty, to God and the Queen, along with the challenge to fill the card and earn the pack lots of money.

For a short spell, dressed in our scout and cub uniforms, we had immunity, freedom to walk up the long gravel drives of the large mansions with impunity. If challenge by a suspicious resident who may have, in the past, confronted us when we were up to no good we could now give a legitimate reason to be on their private land. It was a legitimate reason to trespass, to case the joints for future apple theft in the autumn.

We washed cars, windows, cut grass, weeded borders and numerous odd jobs. Some odder than others. One eccentric householder marched us through his garden to a conservatory, clinging, along with the ivy, to the side of a dilapidated house; the sort of property estate agents would describe as having abundant charm. He had a military bearing and moustache and called us 'chaps' and 'young uns'. The job was to wash a massive pile of flower pots. A pointless task, like painting stones or rocks white on some colonial military base to keep soldiers from boredom. After half-heartedly washing the pots, we received half-hearted praise, "Jolly well done, chaps!" and half a crown. Some people would use us with understandable reluctance; car washing created a mess without a discernible difference to their cars, valued plants dug out of the earth instead of dandelions. I once polished, to the dismay of the owner, not only the uppers, but also the soles of his brogues.

Willie, knocking on one door found himself faced by the very odd and Very Reverend Pyke, a tall, thin, ascetic man, who told him in a sinister voice,

"Do not darken my doorstep ever again!"

On account of his height he was known as Pontop Pike after the radio mast. There was a rumour that he was the brother of the TV personality Magnus Pyke whose media image was that of an eccentric mad scientist. Pontop must have recognised the mad scientist in my brother and concerned for his property, and his life had told him to bugger off.

Memory Spill

Once we had completed a job and whether the householder was satisfied or not, we handed them a 'job done' window sticker. Even as we looked back while closing the gate we would see the relieved householder sticking the sign on the inside of their lounge window thus exempting them from further bothersome visits by Cubs or Scouts.

One of the most memorable jobs was clearing out the store room for our local grocer. Our mother had suggested Mr Scott as a potential customer, or victim. We trooped into his shop across the road and asked if he had any jobs he needed doing. Mr Scott, a kind man but wandered, led us through his shop and a heady combination of aromas: coffee, biscuits, cheese and paraffin, to the back yard of the shop. There, inside a store room, were piles of cardboard and timber boxes. Mr Scott stood in the doorway, as though in a trance, gazing at the stack of boxes.

"Och, I've been meaning to get rid of all these boxes for a wee while."

"We can do that Mr Scott." said Willie. Then a little too eagerly. "We could burn them."

"Aye, you could do that, Willie. That would be a grand help."

Mr Scott had no way of knowing we had, some years before, razed the local railway station to the ground. No way of knowing my brother was an accidental pyromaniac.

We set about stacking the boxes, in a pile that would not disgrace an Indian funeral pyre, with no regard for the restricted dimensions of the yard.

"Look at this," whispered Willie.

We gathered round my brother in the doorway. The removal of the boxes had revealed a large paraffin storage tank with a tap at the front.

Memory Spill

"This'll help get the fire going," said Willie as he filled empty lemonade bottles for us to slosh paraffin over our bonfire.

We looked sideways at Willie; he had said something similar in the bushes at the back of the late Broomieknowe railway station.

The pyre erupted in a fireball which vaporised the telephone wires hanging overhead, then settled down to an inferno, a firestorm, the sort we had seen on a TV documentary about the Blitz. The paint on the doors bubbled and one of the storeroom window panes cracked. Forced by the intense heat we retreated into the far corner of the small yard.

Across the yard, through the flames, Mr Scott appeared. He was standing in the doorway, mesmerized, trying to make sense of it all, a steamy vapour coming off his overall.

"Grand job, aye, grand job lads," said Mr Scott. He then turned and closed the scorched door just before he combusted

We completed the job, tidied up, leaving the yard looking as though the Lunar Landing Module just had blasted off. We walked in to the shop to receive our payment to find Mr Scott standing behind his counter slightly red in the face and his apron lightly toasted. He was chatting to my mother. She turned to look at her two sons and friend, Hallie, smoke damaged and lightly coated with ash. She looked back at Mr Scott, then looked again at us, with a suspicious expression on her face. An expression we were very familiar with.

Tommy Green's final inspirational idea was to build an activity centre in the woods that surrounded Melville Castle. It would stand at the edge of the disused curling pond. As we gathered to listen to our scoutmaster describe his vision my mind wandered back to sometime years before when, one summer, we had a gang hut in the bushes high above on the edge of the woods.

During our explorations of our new domain we had discovered a dilapidated shed containing ancient curling stones. We had carried the heavy stones up through the wood and released them, then stood listening as the stones, that had taken God knows how long to grind and shape in their making, crash though the woods and splash into the pond far below.

Tommy's gang hut would be a more substantial affair than ours. Volunteer parents dug the foundation and filled the shallow trenches with concrete. A borrowed tractor with us scouts bouncing about in a trailer drove to Rosewell, a town quite a few miles away, to collect surplus bricks that Tommy had scrounged. On the way back, we sat on top of the load the sharp edges of the bricks stabbing our arses through the thin fabric of our shorts.

Whether due to a lack of funds or enthusiasm the project lost momentum. After a few courses of brick had been laid on the concrete foundations Tommy's grand project ground to a halt, the overgrown brickwork a sad memorial to Tommy Green's contribution to the community.

In those uncomplicated days, the Scouts, Guides, Cubs and Brownies, like the church and school played an important part in the life of the village. But soon, to the great disappointment of my dad, a King Scout in his youth, I left the Scouts. One dark winter evening, I was climbing the Post Office Steps, on my way home from a Scout meeting.

"Ye heard, Pal?" A voice in the dark.

"Heard what?"

"President Kennedy's gone and been assassinated!"

Memory Spill

It was 7.30 on Friday the 22 November 1963. I went home and sat on my bed in a state of deep shock. At a time when political leaders were old men with grey hair, pipes and moustaches, Jack Kennedy, with his film star looks, was someone we teenagers could relate to. He had celebrity status; a year before we had followed the Cuban Crisis with apprehensive awe.

Life was no longer simple and uncomplicated. Not long after, I drifted away from the Scouts, an organisation that didn't seem relevant in this new world, the world of the swinging 60s.

Memory Spill

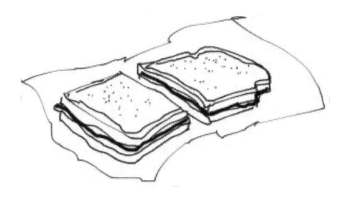

Chapter 11
A Scottish Sandwich

Occasionally, I have used vernacular words: for example, as a child my mother would send me for the 'messages' which in Scotland means the shopping, a daily chore in the days before supermarkets and fridge freezers. This is a short story that explains the word 'piece' when used in a culinary sense by a Scot. It is set in the early 1970s and I had been living in England for a few years. The story is this:

Early in our relationship, I took Ann on a date to see a well-known American singer, David Gates, perform at Leeds Town Hall. It was February and the auditorium was freezing, the victim of a power cut, and everyone was dressed in winter attire, the audience a sea of fur hats. It looked like a Dr Zhivago convention. This was the 1970's the decade of power cuts, miners' strikes and three-day weeks. Followed by more industrial disputes and power cuts.

Gates heroically performed in a thin suit and a shirt with buttons undone to reveal a bare chest, no doubt covered in more goose pimples than hairs. We speculated that he must from Alaska. An equally heroic orchestra provided the music, accompanied by the castanet chatter of teeth. The audience clapped manically at the end of each number, the only way to generate bodily heat.

Periodically, during the performance the man next to Ann climbed over some empty seats in front of us, scuttled along the row and left the hall only to return a few minutes later. When he was not seat hurdling he quietly, and annoyingly, hummed and softly whistled along with the performer. He either had a severe incontinence problem or he was one, or maybe two, notes short of an octave. At first, he was an amusing diversion and Ann and I smiled at each other in the darkness.

As the second half of the show started there was a strange rustling noise from our bizarre neighbour.

"What's he doing now?" asked Ann out of the side of her mouth. I leant forward and peered through the gloom, leant back and whispered out the side of my mouth

"He's got his piece out" I answer. The seats creaked and squeaked as the audience within earshot of my sonorous stage whisper shifted uneasily, the way sheep react when they notice a dog peering with intent through a five-bar gate.

"CHANGE SEATS WITH ME, NOW!" demanded Ann, now rigid with fear, in a much louder stage whisper. We changed seats and I sat next to the oddball as he noisily munched his ham sandwich ... or if you are a recent immigrant from Scotland, a ham piece.

Chapter 12
Child labour

To qualify for pocket money, my dad expected me to do chores in the home and good deeds: gardening, going for messages and suchlike for the elderly neighbours. If I impressed Mrs Fisher or Mr Cook with my efforts at horticulture, I'm not sure. One good deed, walking the Cook's dog Rover, created a desire to have a dog of my own. My mum and dad resisted the idea for a while. My efforts at animal husbandry had not impressed; I had neglected Tag, my hamster, then a guinea pig, and I didn't have much to do with Nicky, our one-eyed cat with the shredded ear. But, my parents relented and found someone with a Border Collie puppy for sale. The price, a bottle of wine from William Scott, Family Grocer and Wine Merchant on the corner on the opposite side of the road from where we lived. The inevitable discussion about a name took place. I liked Buck, the name of the husky in 'Call of the Wild', the Jack London novel I had just read. My father winced when I suggest Fang, based on another of London's novels 'White Fang'. Compromising I agreed to my mum's suggestion: Corrie. It didn't matter. I had a dog, and I was beside myself with joy.

The weeks dragged by, then the day came when, in a state of high excitement I walked across the town to exchange the bottle of wine for Corrie. He was so small he fitted into the front pouch of my anorak as I walked on my way home. Corrie became my constant companion and roamed the neighbourhood at my side apart from the times when, encouraged by me, he terrorised cats.

One day he vanished down a driveway in pursuit of a terrified cat, and as usual I waited on the pavement for him to come back. On this occasion, heralded by the shrieks of the irate cat owner, he reappeared from behind the house and flashed passed me at greyhound velocity.

There was a screech of brakes and a dull thud as Corrie ran straight into the side of a Ford Popular. I turned around to see Corrie sliding down the side of the car revealing an indentation in the driver's door panel. It was the dog shaped dent you see in Tom and Jerry cartoons but with a smear of real blood where the nose had impacted.

I raised my eyes from surveying this catastrophic damage to find arm resplendent with tattoos of anchors and a dagger hung out of the window. The driver must have opened it prior to the impact. It wouldn't open now I thought.

"Is thon dug yours, son?" The face above the arm enquired.

"It is, mister." I couldn't deny ownership. Corrie was leaning against my leg, tongue lolling and cross eyed with a drizzle of blood on his black nose.

"Is yer dug a'right?" said the driver nodding at Corrie. "Ah could have run the poor beast ower."

Memory Spill

Resisting the urge to look at the massive dent I looked into his eyes and thanked him for not ending my dog's life.

As the car puttered off down the road, I put Corrie on his lead intending to flee the scene before the car owner got home and discovered the damage.

"Not so fast, young man!"

It was the cat owner. An irate Mrs Monteith.

Not long after Jimmy Muirhead, the local baker, would mention Mrs Monteith. He was about to give me my first proper, regular job: baker's delivery boy. My brother had pedalled the bike for two years and he had passed his cycle clips down to me. Willie had moved on to greater things; his resignation nothing to do with the incident involving the birthday cake ordered by Mrs Monteith. He had left the cake, secure in its box, at the back door, the tradesman's entrance. By coincidence a local squirrel, also celebrating its birthday, opened the box and consumed most of the cake. He then invited the numerous species of excited birds, resident in the Monteith's extensive, well stocked garden, to his birthday bash. Little remained of the cake, not even enough to stick a candle in.

On my first day in the job, my new boss, Jimmy Muirhead, mentioned this mishap as part of my induction training, an example of something I must on no account do. The induction talk took a considerable time; Jimmy had a habit of repeating things, in fact almost everything he said. As a younger, inquisitive child, I had asked my dad why Mr Muirhead, who lived across the road from us, had a small square shape, like a miniature loft hatch, in his head. Dad told me he had heard Mr Muirhead had suffered a serious head injury, the result of a motorcycle accident, in the days before the wearing of crash helmets was mandatory. As I listen to Jimmy outlining my duties I imagined this small hatch opening

Memory Spill

to reveal a tangle of wires that were sparking and short circuiting causing him to repeat each sentence he uttered.

Following a demonstration in the art of packing bread, buns and cakes into the cardboard boxes, I followed Jimmy out into the street where the delivery bike leant against the wall. The frame of the bike resembled a section of the Forth Bridge with wheels bolted on. There were no gears and moving the bike from a standing start demanded ferocious pumping of the legs.

Having a Saturday job gave me an excuse I could give Peasle, the school PE teacher for not being able to turn out for the rugby B team. I doubt the team missed my rugby skills which were ineffective if non-existent. I hated rugby. Hated running around in the mud chasing a misshapen ball. Hated the steaming scrums with some bastard in the opposing side trying to kick my shins while one of my team mates would let off a disgusting fart in my face. Pedalling Jimmy's museum exhibit bike was a better way to spend Saturday morning.

The customers who ordered deliveries lived at the posh end of Bonnyrigg up a street called Broomieknowe lined with mansions that on one side overlooked the Esk Valley and Lasswade village. Long, crunchy gravel drives led up to the residences. Some, owned by 'Old Money', were in a state of fading elegance and disrepair. The renovated properties owned by 'New Money' had signs directing deliveries to the 'Tradesman's Entrance'. Often 'Old Money' customers would greet me, on a wet winter's day, with sympathy - "You look done in, old chap" - and sometimes even a cup of tea. 'New Money' residents, smug in their new social position were unmoved by the hardship endured by a mere Baker's Boy.

As fate would have it the route to Broomieknowe was a long incline. This demanded energetic pedalling while steering with one hand and using the other to hold in place the cardboard boxes piled in the carrier at the front of the bike.

Memory Spill

The more boxes I could load onto the bike the fewer journeys I needed to make. But the jarring from a pothole or the cobbles of the High Street would often dislodge a box which would fall off the bike and burst open spilling its contents, across the road. If a sliced loaf went under the front wheel, I would have to carry out reconstructive surgery at the roadside or brush road grit off the rolls before reloading the box and making the delivery. It was not unknown for customers visiting the shop during the week to congratulate a puzzled Mrs Muirhead on the interesting 'seeds' adorning the top of the rolls delivered the previous Saturday by the polite Baker's Boy.

Many local characters passed the shop: Sergeant Turner, rumoured to mete out justice in dark alleyways and retired Dr Scott, his panama hat tied to his lapel by a length of string. Dr Scott was so old that his drain pipe trousers and Beatle boots had come back into fashion. But the most colourful character was The Cisco Kid. One day Jimmy was helping me load the bike, or more likely making sure I didn't overload it, as Cisco strolled passed playing his mouth organ. Aged anywhere between twenty-five and forty, and one round short of a six-gun, Cisco was resplendent in his cowboy outfit: a ten-gallon hat, waistcoat, chaps, boots and sheriff's star.

"Och, he's on another planet, on another planet, that one." opined Jimmy.

More likely in Deadwood City, I thought. Where Jimmy and I could see Dr. Somerville approaching in his Rover, Cisco saw a stagecoach rumbling over the cobbles and tumbleweed rolling across the High Street.

"He's the happiest man in Bonnyrigg, the happiest man, son," mused Jimmy, as he eyed me building an unstable ziggurat pyramid of boxes on the front of the bike.

Life was uneventful in the shop, but from time to time there were moments of excitement.

Memory Spill

"Snell, snell!" A pause, "Snell, snell!" Jimmy's excited, loud voice emanated from the front shop.

I was in the back room packing bread and cakes into the cardboard boxes with Jimmy's wife, Mary. Startled by this commotion I resisted the urge to hide under the table. The night before I'd been to the Regal cinema to see Von Ryan's Express, one of the latest war films, which had a lot of German soldiers running around shouting "Schnell! Schnell!" in loud, excited voices at everyone who wasn't a German.

Jimmy marched into the back room. "Did you hear that son? Did you hear that son?"

"Hear what, Mr Muirhead?" I said.

"Old Mrs Kay, old Mrs Kay, she said to me. 'It's snell this morning'. Snell!"

I looked up from trying to squash a loaf into a ridiculously tight space in a box and peered at the hatch in his head. Had the wires shorted again?

"Snell, Mr Muirhead?"

"Aye. Snell, snell, it's the auld Scots for cold son, for cold, son," said Jimmy enlightening me. "I've no' heard that for years, no' heard it for years!"

Neither had Mrs Muirhead, who paused packing a box and rolled her eyes to look up at the ceiling and the flickering fluorescent.

I can't recall how many years I worked for Jimmy, but when I was about 16, and about to leave school I had handed my notice in. This saved Jimmy the trouble of sacking me following an unfortunate lapse in customer care.

On a wet, cold and blustery morning I had just made the final delivery of the day and was about to head back to the shop. I pumped the pedals with my aching legs trying to create the impetus to move the delivery bike wheels which had become bogged down in the deep gravel and head back to the shop.

"Baker's boy! Baker's boy!" A loud piping voice accompanied by crunching gravel.

I turned mid-thrust on the pedals, rain, mingling with sweat, dripping of the end of my nose, to see a small boy, a pupil of one of the Edinburgh public schools, resplendent in an immaculate school uniform and cap. "I say, Baker's Boy, Baker's Boy, mummy would like.........."

Being called a Baker's Boy by this Little Lord Fauntleroy was just too much to bear. It offended my adolescent communist leanings.

"Fuck off, sonny!" I muttered.

Startled, the distressed boy ran back down the long gravel drive, eager to regale mummy with the strange turn of phrase used by the 'Baker's Boy' while I pedalled back to face Jimmy's disappointment. In duplicate.

I must have left on good terms as later, older and wiser, during my Easter holidays from College, I made deliveries in Jimmy's Ford Anglia van which had superseded the bike.

There were other occasional opportunities for employment during weekends. My friend Rob Gillies lived on a farm in the countryside outside Lasswade where his dad looked after the cattle. Through his contacts in the farming community he knew a bloke who organised bird shoots for local businessmen masquerading as toffs. He needed beaters. It sounded interesting and the money would come in handy. One frosty Saturday morning I met Rob up at the farm and we set off to the shoot as a watery orange sun surfaced above the misty fields.

We found the other beaters in a clearing under a cloud of feathery cold breath mingled with cigarette smoke, huddled together like Emperor penguins seeking meagre communal warmth. Everything, the trees, fence posts and the fields were white with frost and clouds scudded across the grey sky driven by the chilling wind.

"Right, you lot listen tae me. I am the gamekeeper, Mr McTaggart."

At the sound of the loud voice the group turned to find a small, wind eroded man with a fierce beard and a large stick in his hand. He had appeared without a sound, not even the crack of a twig.

"Your task, lads, is to drive the wildlife from the undergrowth and the gorse towards the gentlemen with the guns. Dinnae, under any circumstances go past the brow of yon hill. Half the bastards are just as likely to shoot one o' yoos as a fuckin' bird."

At this we all shuffled sheep like, very aware of our mortality.

"Whit you've t' dae is this," said the gamekeeper, swinging his stick and thrashing a nearby bush.

"KAH, KAH, KAH!" He shouted at the top his voice. "KAH, KAH, KAH!"

Startled, I stepped back onto the foot of the beater behind.

"Fuckin' watch it pal."

Each beater armed with a stick took up their position in the line. I found myself at the end next to Rob.

In a cacophony of shouting, the line moved towards the edge of the wood driving startled birds, pheasants and partridges, flapping into the cold air, towards the sharp sound of gunfire and lead shot that bounced around the tree canopy.

At lunch time, we gathered around a battered Land Rover to eat our lunch; cheese pieces washed down with sweetened tea. Across the other side of the clearing the shooters enjoyed a better culinary spread washed down with whisky. They struck poses and conversed in loud important voices as they viewed their meagre tally of dead birds, imaging themselves on a shoot in a picturesque glen on some Braemar estate.

I didn't go on any more shoots; the pointless slaughter of pheasants and partridges for amusement didn't appeal to me.

In the summer of 1966, after I had left school, and, before I attended college, I had worked at the local concrete works. My first job was operating a guillotine cutting blocks of concrete into mock stone of different hues and dimensions, then promoted to making concrete lintels of doubtful structural integrity. But, the Christmas holiday soon loomed, and my entertainment schedule required money. Seeking a holiday job, I offered my services to Mrs Smith, the postmistress who ran Lasswade village post office.

Her doubtful eyes peered over the counter top. She was remembering me as a troublesome boy, one half of the Wilson brothers; recalling incidents involving fireworks, stink bombs and broken windows.

She had once watched, from her back-office window, as we recycled lemonade bottles from the unlocked store of the local Grocer and 'Italian Warehouseman' in the alley below. By recycle, I mean we stole the empty bottles, took them into the shop, inhaled the smell of ground coffee and other exotic foodstuffs and claimed the two pence return payment. The proprietor, Mrs Black in the grip of the early onset of dementia, failed to realise that we had, ten minutes before, handed in the same bottles. Mrs Black would then wander up the path to deposit the bottles back in her unlocked store. And so, the process went on, until, in the way of village life, Mrs Smith gave the heads up to my granny, who lived just up the road from the Post Office. The scam was stamped out with minimal fuss. So, my honesty, essential to a member of staff of a successful Post Office, was tarnished.

But Mrs Smith's husband, a hard looking but kindly man. Ignorant of my childhood misdemeanours, saw a pleasant young man, a veteran baker's delivery boy and grandson of Mrs Walter, a regular customer and son of Jim Wilson, Church Elder and Treasurer. The job was mine.

On my first day, I turned up dressed in my WW1 full length leather flying coat that I had found hung in a cupboard in my granny's house, a trapper hat and college scarf. This was my winter college outfit. I thought it was 'cool', defining me as a modish design student. Mr Smith, looked me up and down like a diner expecting a succulent steak, but served a plate of whelks.

"Jings! Whit Soviet Gulag have you escaped from, son?" he said with an uncertain smile, failing to see the trend setting design student.

My first task was sorting mail in the back office. It was from here in this room that Mrs Smith had looked down on our bottle scam, and decades before, in the summer of 1917, a telegram would have passed through, bringing the devastating news to my family, of the death of my grandfather, Clem, at the Battle of Arras. One telegram among many.

After a mail sorting session, I met Jimmy Jones for the first time. Each temporary worker partnered a regular postman and mine would be Jimmy. We stepped out of the door on our first joint mission into a small snow storm. Out of earshot of the management, Jimmy caught my arm.

"Listen, son," said Jimmy, "'ah dinnae want ye tae gang aroond yer half o' the roond like Eric Liddell."

"Eric who, Mr Jones?" The film Chariots of Fire was a long way into the future.

Memory Spill

"Liddell. A runner, son, a famous runner," Jimmy enlightened me, adding with Scottish pride, "a Scottish runner." Then, getting to the point. "The boy last year got back more than an 'oor afore me. Made me look slaw, y'ken."

There was a constant fear time and motion inspectors, rumoured to carry out clandestine inspections, with dire consequences for any postman dawdling.

"Well, Mr Jones, why don't we fix a time to meet up, then we'll go into the Post Office together?" I suggested in a show of worker solidarity.

"That sounds grand, son. And dinnae ca' me Mr Jones, ca' me Jimmy." And so, we began a partnership that would last four years.

Jimmy was at least sixty, on his last legs I thought from my vantage point of 17 years old. I agreed to take the longer half of the round that started with some timber clad dwellings known as the Swedish Houses, then up to the local sandpit and down through the Melville estate to the Castle. From there I followed a track to deliver to several farms before ending up at Dobbies Nursery. A long, long walk. A long walk, but with few letters. I only had about forty letters and, every Thursday, a strange, small package with the weight of anti-matter for the Sandpit. The largest number of the letters had the address of a bungalow near to the nursery. They were from every part of the globe. As I stood in a cloud of frosty breath, feeding the letters through the slot, I would imagine the senders addressing the envelopes and licking stamps in warmer, faraway sunny places: Brazil, Mexico, Portugal and India.

The latter half of the 60s was the time when the government experimented with not turning the clocks back for winter. Scotland, far north of the seat of government in London, was in darkness until mid-morning. I started work at six o'clock in the dark and finished my first shift, still in darkness, at about half past ten. I would walk through the silent countryside, along the hard-rutted farm tracks, through a dark tunnel of trees, in snow and frost, the frozen puddles silver pools in the moonlight, singing to myself; 'My Generation', Bonzo Dog's 'I'm the urban spaceman' and the Beatles 'Please, Mr Postman'

"Mr Postman, oh yeah, wait a minute, wait a minute, Mr Postman, deliver the letter, the sooner the better............"

In the blackness I would sometimes bump into a farm worker, and, one morning the pale silhouette of a large pig crossed the track in front of me. A scary moment; I had read in a newspaper of an attack by a porker of such a size on a woman. It had almost chewed her arm off. I froze, stopped singing about postmen and watched as the pig slipped into the undergrowth.

With my part of the round completed I had to kill at least an hour in the freezing cold so that I could coordinate my rendezvous with Jimmy. I would find a secluded clearing in the woods of Melville Estate, build a large fire and sit reading a book with a flask of coffee and a couple of pieces with ham or cheese by my side. Then it was back to the post office where I would walk in with Jimmy, shaking snow off my leather flying coat. Mr and Mrs Smith standing behind the counter would watch our arrival with narrow eyed suspicion.

Memory Spill

All good things come to an end, they say. Even now, after many decades I still look back with fondness on my days as a Christmas postman. Many times, in my life, in stressful moments, I have wished myself back to that simple life, walking through the snow-covered countryside, under a canopy of twinkling stars and steady planets.

But before my stint as a Christmas Postman I had to complete the last leg of my education at Lasswade Secondary School.

Memory Spill

Chapter 13
Secondary School

There was a loud bang. In an explosion of chalk dust, a small dull metal coin, a three pence piece, shot up in the air. Twenty pairs of upturned eyes followed the spinning coin then tracked it as it fell back onto the still quivering desk

This was my introduction to Secondary School. Before we sat down at our desks, our teacher had told us to gather around his desk. We waited in a hushed state of expectation as he pulled open a drawer on the far side. From the drawer, he took a threepenny coin and a thick leather belt, the dreaded tawes, and laid the two items on the desktop. Nobody dared interrupt him to ask the purpose of all this. We were like a small invited audience watching a magician laying out his props.

He placed the coin in the middle of the desk, flexed the thick belt, and then with a sudden swing of his arm struck the coin with the belt.

Memory Spill

We stared at the rotating coin as it slowed to settled on the desktop covered with the indentations of coins used in previous years. Returning to our desks we knew not to cross Mr Roberts, which was the purpose of the demonstration. I returned to my desk and sat down with a sense of doom. Mr Roberts was our maths teacher. I well knew of my shortcomings in arithmetic, the essential foundations of mathematics. Having experienced the thumbscrews of multiplication and long division I was about to be painfully stretched on the rack of algebra and logarithms.

The Comprehensive Secondary school, was a grey, grim building that sprawled on the edge of the town. It would not have looked out of place in East Germany. I had felt at ease at the small village Primary School with its easier pace of life, and I had felt comfortable knowing I had been walking in the footsteps of my ancestors. To increase my discomfort, my mother had sent me to the new school in shorts, a fashion faux pas. It could have been a worse; I might have turned up at school in my kilt and sporran. The situation continued through the autumn term until, before Christmas, in a snow-covered playground, some older boys jumped me and stuffed snow up the legs of my shorts. Later, sitting in the classroom with uncomfortable frozen testicles, I resolved to persuade my mother to buy me a pair of long trousers. The following week I appeared at school in a more confident frame of mind in my new Co-op store grey long trousers.

By a quirk of fate, the Government had decreed that pupils of my year of Primary School would not take the 11 plus exam. I doubt I would have coped with the stress of such a crucial exam, so I imagine was pleased to miss it. There were three certificate classes and three general classes. Certificate meant that the authorities expected pupils in even the lowlier 'C' classes to get at least two O Levels. The General Class pupils trained on the tools they would wield when they left school at 15 years old ready take up a trade. I found myself in class C3, the lowest certificate class. This year would be unlike previous years. Instead of French the C3 class would learn woodwork, metalwork and technical drawing. Skills to fall back on if we failed to gain any O Levels. My dad, who considered being able to speak in a foreign tongue a vital life skill was en colère. Which, for those like me who took the technical subjects, I think means 'angry'.

My father had attended George Heriot's School in Edinburgh, a prestigious private school that the more affluent residents of the town sent their kids to. If his youngest son was to be denied the opportunity to learn French in the Comprehensive system, he would pay to have him educated. I took a day off from the humble state school and attended the entrance exam. I sat at a Victorian desk in a musty neo-gothic hall and stared with incomprehension at the questions on the paper in front of me. It was no surprise to hear I had I failed. The whole episode had been an ordeal, and it was a relief to be back, if not with Mr Roberts the maths teacher, at least with my friends. My father, less happy, accepted my failure with his usual good grace and he never again mentioned my lack of French language. But I have noticed that everyone I knew who learned French never seemed to speak the language once they left school whereas the technical skills that gained I came in handy in my career as a designer.

Class C3 was an all-boys class. As we laboured in front of a furnace in the metalworking class or planed lumps of wood in the joinery workshop, our female counterparts were honing their domestic skills. The class had a monitor who carry the class attendance book from class to class. The monitor would present the book to each teacher who would carry out a head count and record any absentees. This could be a tricky responsibility. Big Murch, a large and intimidating classmate liked to be absent; a lot. He expected the monitor of the week to hand the unwary teacher a pencil to mark his absence. This meant that the monitor could rub out the incriminating mark. Cooperation in this sleight of hand was mandatory as it was better to be a mate of Big Murch than an enemy. Some teachers, Mr Roberts being one, would smile at the nervous monitor and wave the proffered pencil away and use a ball point pen. Mr Robert's betrothed the less savvy Toy Balloons who us taught English would accept the proffered soft pencil. As the term progressed Big Murch and other frequent AWOL members of class would schedule their absences to coincide with the users of the soft pencil.

Toy Balloons, was an inspirational teacher. She held our testosterone infused pubescent attention during the lesson. This was in part due to her magnificent breasts but was also an excellent teacher. Apart from her bosom, I still remember the words of Ode to Autumn by Keats. Well maybe not all of them. She encouraged us to find the imagery in poetry and prose; to enjoy the written word. There were many other good teachers. The teachers in the technical classes were demanding but fair. Jock Glass who taught technical drawing and Eckie Rollo who taught us to make household items out of wood and metal had been tradesmen in another life and were more down to earth and less vulnerable than the more academic teachers to the abuse of unruly teenagers. Like many schoolchildren my opinion of individual teachers stemmed from my ability or inability at a subject. I was useless at maths and therefore my relationship with Mr Roberts was dire. Another subject I loathed was Physical Education. My dodgy lungs ensured I was not an enthusiastic participant in any sport. I must have been a disappointment to the P.E. Teacher Mr Stewart or 'Peasle', as he known behind his back. I formed the opinion that Peasle thought he was still training marines or commandos for the Normandy landings, not delicate school boys. But, now as I look back the uncompromising physical gym lessons, the treks in the Grampians with Baxter Cooper and the cold mornings pedalling the baker's delivery bike were the foundation for the health I enjoy today.

One afternoon we arrive at the gym and trudged into the changing rooms. We changed and sat on the slatted benches surrounded by the fug of rubber gym shoes, stale sweat and a hint of piss from the toilets. Peasle marched in with a young man with an intense eager expression and dressed in a crisp Daz white kit.

"Right, boys. This is Hugh. He's a student teacher, and he's taking you for this lesson," said Peasle, then outlined the dire consequences of failing to obey the novice teacher before leaving him standing in the centre of the room under our hostile scrutiny.

Call me "Hugh" hailed from England, the auld enemy. With commendable enthusiasm he declared his intention to teach us cricket, a game we Scots were not familiar with. We were in equal measure intrigued by this new game and fascinated by Hugh's posh English accent. But most of all relieved to miss out on a lesson from Peasle.

Addressing us as "chaps" Hugh launched into an eager description of the game; the relevance of the stumps, how to wield a bat and the material construction of the ball. Using a diagram stuck to the changing room door he pointed, like a general, to the various positions around the space between the stumps: deep cover, square leg and short leg. Silly mid-off got a guffaw. Boredom descended; Tooter Ritchie started a mock brawl with Scud Kemp and someone at the back sang "Hey, Hey, Hugh, Hugh, get off my cloud"; a play on the current Rolling Stones hit single. Sensing he was losing the dressing room Hugh cut the talk short and led us out onto the playing fields.

Not the playing fields of Eton that Hugh was more familiar with. With the backdrop of the unimaginative school buildings this was more like the playing fields of some drab East German communist block 'schule'. As we walked across the threadbare grass Hugh threw the cricket ball around amongst us 'chaps'.

"Jings!" exclaimed Tooter catching the ball, "it's like a wee fuckin' cannon ba'! Can we no use a tennis ba' like when we play roonders, Hugh?"

Hugh pondered on this foreign outburst as he pounded the stumps into the sun-baked ground.

"Right, ho, chaps, choose someone to bat!"

Realising that this was like volunteering to be at the wrong end of a firing squad we stood looking down at our gym shoes or staring across the playing field at the grey communist block style council houses that surrounded the school.

"Fudge, yer in, yer battin'."

Volunteered by Big Murch, who by dint of his size was the class spokesman, Fudge Fowler trudged up to the wicket and stood with a look of hopeless resignation tinged with fear, as Hugh polished the ball vigorously on the crotch of his white shorts. Meanwhile we positioned ourselves at square leg, deep cover and silly mid-off. Silly mid-off? We might as well have been miles off. We had no intention at all of catching this deadly projectile. In the event, there was nothing to catch.

Hugh gave the ball one last rub on his crotch, then bounded up to the crease, a gazelle on the Serengeti. As he bowled his arm was almost invisible scything arc. The released ball bounced on the brown grass with a puff of dust. Fudge, in desperation swung the bat and missed. There was no thwack of leather on willow, only an 'oomph' on abdomen. Fudge staggered, stumbled and fell back scattering the stumps and bails to lie on his back like a dead hen.

Skud shouted "Yer oot, Fudge!" And he was 'oot'. Well and truly out of it for some time.

I had always owned a bike but the journey to and from the village school was by foot; the Big Brae, the Wee Brae and the School Brae would have tested the most experienced Tour de France rider. As a family, we would often ride out to the numerous beauty spots in the region, some far away. The roads, in the 1950s were quiet at weekends and cycling was a safe and leisurely activity. Unlike the route to the Primary School the roads leading to the Secondary School were flat and so the mode of transport to and from school was the bicycle. My brother and I and all our friends had second-hand bikes. How Hodgson's bike shop in the centre of the town survived I've no idea. All we ever bought were accessories and coloured tape and transfers to titivate our 'previously owned' bikes. The school ran a cycle proficiency course for eager bikers to keep the road casualty figures down. We were eager bikers but not that eager.

Every so often there would be an unannounced raid on the bike shed by Sergeant Turner and a fresh-faced constable who would pick out the bikes with worn tyres, worn brakes and other defects and throw them in a pile. A large pile. We would stream out of school, heads full of dreams and plans for the evening, only to stop and stare at the metal mountain. While the smug Proficiency Badge holders cycled out of the gate, we had to disentangle our bikes and present ourselves to Sergeant Turner who would point out the defect or defects. Clutching a ticket, we would walk our bikes out of the school until out of sight of the police and cycle home. The days after a police raid would see a spike in sales of the more sensible accessories at Hodgson's bike shop: new tyres, brake blocks and reflectors.

Christmas was close, and the annual school dance was on the horizon. The year before, the organisers had pandered to the new Pop Music culture. As the music of the Rolling Stones, the Kinks and the Animals throbbed around the Assembly Hall, the pupils had gravitated into two distinct groups; boys on one side of the hall, girls on the other. We posed and postured, preening ourselves like mating birds while glancing with studied nonchalance at the girls on the other side of the empty dance floor. The atmosphere in the Hall was an unhealthy fug of slight sweat, cheap perfume and our father's Old Spice aftershave.

Peasle our PE teacher decided this would not happen again. This year he would train us not only to dance but to dance with aplomb. Peasle was about to reveal a warm, human side to his character that some of us believed to be non-existent. This would be a Christmas dance to remember.

We were sitting in the changing room as usual in our sweat stained shorts and vests. As always there was a palpable tension in the fetid air. Some of us had noticed the faint bloodstains on Ronnie Proc's kit and were reliving his screams, when, during the previous lesson he had trapped his head between the springs of the trampoline, Peasle's latest piece of apparatus. Ronnie's ears almost lost his ears in the process of releasing him. As we sat pondering on what lay in store for us, the dulcet tones of "Chattanooga Choo Choo" seeped into the changing room and swirled around, mingling with the smell of the unique aroma of well used gym shoes.

"Whit the fuck's that......?"

The changing room door swung open with a bang against a bench as Peasle marched in and turned in the centre of the room with military precision, as if on castors, to face the author of the profanity.

"That, Murchison is music. Melodious music, you moron."

"Sir, sir!" called an excited voice from the far side of the room, "That's alliteration, Sir!"

At least one of us had listened to Toy Balloons during English class. The room fell silent and thirty buttocks clenched. Such a display of being clever could earn the culprit two circuits of the rugby pitch in the late November drizzle or, if it was a nice day, fifty press ups with Peasle's foot on his neck.

But Peasle was in a trance; absent, his eyes glazed over, lost in the undulating music. In his mind he may have been in some far-off WW2 theatre of war, dancing in a Nissan Hut to Swing Music with a pretty nurse or Wren.

The distant music ended, and the gramophone needle squeaked and scraped. Peasle snapped out of his reverie.

"That, Murchison," he said with reverence, "was Glen Miller's Big Band."

"D'ye mean like The Troggs?" asked Big Murch recklessly before adding, "Sir!"

"The who?"

"No The Who Sir, The Troggs. They're a band, ye ken, like The Who." Big Murch endeavoured to bring Peasle up to date with the current Pop scene. "And, they're big, the noo."

Memory Spill

Born later, in another era, Big Murch would have been a fan of the Sex Pistols or perhaps head banged to heavy metal music.

The changing room again tensed at this exchange. But Peasle emitted a slow, resigned sigh of someone that had listened to, but did not comprehend, an obscure scientific theory. He shook his head and asked us to assemble in the gym where he would teach us to dance. To dance with poise and finesse.

We trooped into the gym and lined up in front blood-stained canvas of the trampoline. Bouncing around on the trampoline was no longer regarded as fun.

Peasle stood arms akimbo facing us. "Right, pay attention!" he barked. "Today, you will learn to dance. Proper dancing, not jerking around like demented puppets!"

"Ah thought we were playin' Murder Ba', Sir." This was Big Murch, sounding like Jim Taggart at a crime scene, asking if we would play Murder Ball, his favourite indoor game.

The clue was in the name. The game began when a large leather ball, filled with what felt like sand was placed in the middle of the gym floor between two opposing teams who strove, by any means, to carry the ball to the opposite end of the room. There were few clear rules and many injuries. Based on selection by height, Big Murch fronted one team and I the other. It was like facing Attila the Hun at the apex of a phalanx of bloodthirsty soldiers. Many of us still nursed a catalogue of injuries from the previous week's fixture.

Ignoring Big Murch, Peasle separated us into two groups, one to represent the girls, the other group the boys. Once the protest from the group designated as the girls died down, Peasle marched over to the gramophone and bent over to place the needle on the spinning disc. After a few seconds of hissing, "In the Mood" flowed gently around the room.

Memory Spill

"I will now show you what I expect." Peasle announced as he picked one of the smaller, more athletic of the 'girls' and launched into a waltz, manoeuvring the embarrassed pupil around the polished parquet floor with impressive skill.

We watched, astonished at this revelation of Peasle's feminine side. Then we tried to emulate this exposition of 'proper dancing'. We stumbled about, standing on toes and colliding with each other, laughter and curses almost drowning out the music. But, our skills improved, and order replaced chaos. Every week Peasle alternated the roles of each group. He must have watched Steptoe and Son, the popular TV comedy of the time about the fractious relationship between a father and son. In one episode Harold Steptoe's father, to his surprise, helps him prepare for taking a new girlfriend to a social event, by teaching him dance routines. But in the training sessions Harold always took the female role, the father, his mentor, the male dancer. With acute embarrassment Harold's relationship hits the rocks on the dance floor when he realises he cannot dance as the male partner.

As the weeks progressed and the School Dance loomed our repertoire of dance genres expanded to include The Gay Gordons, Canadian Barn dancing and Scottish Country Dancing. Then, to our relief girls joined us for the lessons. Introducing the fairer sex brought into focus etiquette, the essential ingredient of dancing. Against all expectations Peasle had created a genuine enthusiasm for dance and Big Murch no longer mentioned Murder Ball.

The evening of the dance arrived. I had a shower, or stood under the dribble of warm water that fell from the shower head at the end of its journey through the rubber pipes connected to the bath taps. Then after dressing myself and applying Clearasil to my spots, I looked at myself in the full-length mirror. I felt confident and 'with it'. The shirt collar with the stud and the tie with the horizontal stripes looked modern. Influenced by Brian Jones and George Harrison I had been allowing my hair to grow hoping my mother wouldn't notice and insist on a visit to Mr McKenzie for a short back and sides. But I thought it could do with a bit of tidying up. In the bathroom cabinet I found the ideal gadget which mum had bought from the door salesman: a comb with an integrated razor blade. I didn't bother to read the instructions on the box; it was obvious how to use it, just drag the device through your hair. If Michelangelo, poised to make an incision with a two-inch chisel on back of David's head, had sneezed the Statue of David would have had a similar gap in his hair. Mine looked like a small parking bay suitable for a Dinky car. I lifted the chunk off blond hair off my shoulder and stared at it in mute horror; should I try gluing it back on?

"Whits happened tae t' back o' yer heid?" said a voice behind me.

We were filing in through the main entrance doors to the school. I turned to give the standard riposte: 'Pish off'. Then we flowed in, through the rotunda into the assembly hall. At first, we formed into the usual gender groups and gazed at each other across the dance floor. I positioned myself at the back of the mob to conceal my hair disaster. We all shifted uncertainly as the record player stylus hissed across a vinyl disc and music filled the hall, drowning out the hum of conversation. Then one of the more confident boys; the school beau, his hair swept up in the soon to be outmoded Rock 'n Roll style approached one of the more glamorous girls and swept her around the dance floor.

"Come on son, get on with it!" I jumped and turned around. It was Peasle, whispering in my ear while staring with raised eyebrows at my mutilated hair.

Soon, the floor was a mass of swirling dancers as the orchestral sound of 'In the Mood' and 'Moonlight Serenade' filled the hall followed by the more chaotic and energetic Scottish Reels and Canadian Barn Dances. Then as the evening drew to a close us we danced the twist and the shake to the Stones, the Kinks and the Beatles. Or as Peasle described with sarcasm, jerk around like demented puppets.

Peasle had taught us the discipline of formal dancing in an almost militaristic way and in the way of teenagers we would never have admitted enjoying the Christmas Dance. But, Peasle had something; dancing to Pop Music required little etiquette or normal human interaction, unless it was a dance to slow music, which was adolescent foreplay with clothes on. The ballroom room style of dancing encouraged, required, manners and respect for the partner you were dancing with. Country dancing, the Scottish Reels and Canadian Barn Dances, fostered a true communal spirit, something that had been missing from previous school dances.

Art was the one subject I enjoyed. I had a natural gift; I was not brilliant at art, but I had a gift none the less. Whereas, a gift for mathematics, science and physical education was absent. The head of the art department, on the cusp of retirement, was Mr Russell assisted by a younger art teacher, Baxter Cooper. The other, Fanny Black, a name to conjure with, retired not long after I arrived. Mr Russell, a rotund man, we called Tubby Russell, Mr Cooper was Coop and as for Miss Black, I dread to think.

Tubby was an excellent watercolour painter and had some of his works displayed in frames on the art classroom wall. If we were doing life drawing, he would stand at my shoulder and with a slightly lecherous tone in his voice he would describe the form of the female breast lying beneath the folds of the reluctant model's blouse. The model, a schoolgirl borrowed from another class, would squirm with unease, her cheeks glowing, as we discuss her intimate, hidden charms in precise anatomical detail. But Mr Cooper was the teacher we spent most of our time with.

Coop was my favourite teacher. Everyone, even pupils with no artistic ability regarded Coop with affection and respect. I can see him now, sitting at his desk, drawing an ink illustration of a hawk or kestrel, for the Scottish Field magazine, pausing to look up, eyes swivelling above his shaggy beard checking we were hard at work too.

One morning he brought an injured owl into the class. He had found it by the side of the road. Like any good teacher, Coop abandoned his lesson plan and used the opportunity to discuss the life of owls. Holding the struggling bird, he pointed to its features; the claws, beak and eyes. He encouraged us to hold the bird too and feel the texture of the feathers and its beating heart. Coop was an enthusiastic amateur ornithologist. Driven by this enthusiasm he started an after-school club. My friend Rob and I were two of the first members of the Lasswade High School Ornithology Club.

The ornithology club met once a week, and we learned about British birds, their habits and their habitats. Besides these meetings Coop would organise weekend field trips; to sunlit nature reserves on the edge of the Firth of Forth, dark woods and frosty fields around Bonnyrigg and Lasswade. We would stand bird spotting and counting the numbers of the various species. These Saturday bird watching field trips were an excellent excuse to avoid the weekend horrors of the rugby field.

My dad, keen to fuel to my new enthusiasm, took me to a second-hand shop in a back street of Edinburgh to buy me a pair of binoculars. At the counter, we studied the various sizes and styles of binoculars, discussed the magnifications then went out into the street to try them out on unsuspecting shoppers. We settled on a pair and the bus home I sat with the leather case hung round my neck. Armed with my second-

Memory Spill

hand binoculars I would watch lapwings, kestrels, buzzards, blue tits, coal tits and the magnificent pair of tits belonging to the girl across the road. At 9.30 every Sunday morning she would open her curtains with a theatrical flourish and stand in front of her bedroom window and lift her nightdress over her head. Then she would dress in her bra and panties before a frock sliding down her body brought the show to an end. Her house was some distance away, but my binoculars brought everything into much sharper focus than the naked eye.

During the school holidays Coop would arrange trips to the Highlands where we would stay in Youth Hostels at Kingussie, Blair Atholl and Pitlochry. I remember experiencing a slight apprehension; I still wet the bed occasionally, and from time to time had blood curdling nightmares. Nightmares I would share with everybody within earshot. Once, on a family jaunt with my father and brother I had woken everyone in a Youth Hostel. The hostel manager, thinking a vile murder was being committed on his watch had fallen down the stairs in his panic. The next morning, he had waved us goodbye with his left hand, his right arm supported in a sling. He seemed happy to see us leave.

But, I remember the field trips as happy times. I can recall Coop coming out of a forest of Douglas Firs holding an Adder by the tail, waving it about to our, and the adder's, alarm. Or, he would pick up a piece of hawk shit, break it apart, and poke about and pick out bits of bones of the rodents that the bird had eaten. On another occasion, we gathered around Coop on the scree of a Highland hillside as he again poked his forefinger into a pile of shit. This time it was deer dung to predict, by the warmth of the shit, how far ahead the herd we were following was. We viewed all this with disgust.

One night during a trip Coop caught my friend Rob, in the hostel dormitory, reading, or, in reality, staring mesmerised at a copy of Titbits, a magazine. As the name suggests the magazine contained pictures of lascivious bare-chested women. Snatching the magazine from Rob's grasp he berated him. "You infantile minded, boy. You will go blind!" said Coop trying to sound annoyed.

The next day Rob redeemed himself by spotting a jay as it flew across a path we were tramping along. Rob had impressed Coop by not only spotting the bird, but knowing the species. Like an Apache Chief naming a brave, he honoured Rob with the name 'Jay Spotter' the Titbits incident forgiven.

Coop's sense of pleasure at Rob's twitching skills was soon to plummet, like a sparrow hawk descending on a hapless rodent. A few days later, on the same trip, after a break to scoff our pieces, we were walking down a rough track that ran along the bottom of a small glen.   After a while, Rob and I striding along, had pulled away from the straggling group. We were chatting away, about the charms of my neighbour's daughter or something along these lines, when with a screeching and a thudding, like a carpet being rhythmically beaten by my granny, a Golden Eagle rose from the heather covered hillside. It was twenty feet from us. If a double decker bus had launched itself into the air, we would have been no less astonished. It was an awesome vision of breath-taking beauty and power.

Memory Spill

Coop, leading the main body of the party around a bend, two hundred yards behind us, just had time to see the Golden Eagle disappear into the distance languidly flapping its enormous wings. We waited in a state of high excitement for everyone to catch us up. But Coop didn't share our excitement. We had, by walking so far ahead, spooked a magnificent and rare bird, denying everyone else the experience of a lifetime.

"You, you.... you... fffu...complete idiots!" he spluttered trying to keep a professional grip on his temper and his language. Coop must have forgiven me; he made sure I would leave school with a good portfolio of art and a reference which would soon prove crucial.

I entered my final year at school with mixed emotions; relief it was almost over but with a gnawing feeling of uncertainty. I had always been the youngest in my class and after my lacklustre attempt at O Levels I stayed on for an extra year to see if I could increase my tally, but only added Higher Art to my meagre list of qualifications. I spent a lot of that long year avoiding Peasle by hiding in Mr Marjoribanks classroom cupboard with Rob Gillies. Marjoribanks, a history teacher obsessed with Roman Britain had caught our imagination. We even went on a couple of memorable, unofficial trips to Hadrian's Wall in his VW camper van.

The end of that year was played out with the production of Gilbert and Sullivan's opera The Mikado. The setting was the mythical town of Titipu, a name which exercised our infantile minds. And Pish-Tush, well I won't go there. It was the grand project of Mr Elrick the music teacher who, like Ko-Ko The Lord High Executioner of Titipu, had a little list: a list of singers to train and things to do. I couldn't sing but I wielded a paintbrush. The Art Department created designs for posters and we larked about painting the scenery flats to the background music as orchestra and choir rehearsed. It was a

Spill

fabulous production. Needless to say, some of us mucked about. We found a ladder to the loft where we would sit around a hatch and drop small balls of paper and matchsticks on the choir. It's a wonder nobody fell through the hatch onto the stage. But I did fall in love with a girl in the second row of the choir. My Yum-Yum. Later at a school dance I plucked up the courage to ask her out while we danced as the Bee Gees sang the evocative 'Massachusetts'. It was a short-lived romance with a long recuperation. When I remember that last year at school I hear the plaintive song from the Mikado 'The Moon and I' in my head.

Soon it was time for the mandatory interview with a visiting Careers Advisor; an attempt to guide pupils towards a career path suited to their skills and qualifications.

The careers advisor had peered at me through the thick lenses of his wire-framed glasses thinking there wasn't much potential in the scruffy pale schoolboy sitting on the other side of the table.

"Art, English and technical drawing." He listed my pathetic total of O Levels. Then, "ah, Higher Art." He said this with the slightly surprised tone of a prospector finding a small grain of gold in his pan.

"Yeah." I said

"Ordnance Survey, map drawing?" he said, "What do you think?"

There was an extended pause. I could hear Spider Webster, the headmaster berating an unfortunate pupil in the corridor. The career advisor tapped the end of his pen on the table top hoping that the next pupil waiting outside the door would be of a higher calibre, someone he could steer towards an exciting and meaningful career. The noise of the tapping pen startled me.

Memory Spill

"Yeah, I'll think about it." I said without enthusiasm.

I didn't think about it. With hindsight, maybe I should have. Mundane stuff, but compensated by a secure pension at the end of my working life. But, somehow, I suspected some level of competence in maths would be an essential requisite of the job, otherwise half of the population would end up wandering about the country lost, baffled by my maps.

So, aged sixteen and in bright summer sunshine I walked down the school drive for the last time. Relieved to be leaving, but apprehensive; I had no idea at all about what to do with the rest of my life.

Memory Spill

Chapter 14
Technical College

A t home at the tea table, dad had put his knife and fork down and looked over his foul-smelling herring at me, slight despair dulling his eyes
.   "I could talk to someone at the Bank. Get you in somewhere."

He was talking about the Royal Bank of Scotland where he worked. "But, they wouldn't thank me. With your numerical skills, the bank would go bust!". Years into the future someone with far greater understanding of finance than his son would bring the Royal Bank down: Fred the Shred. It would have mortified my dad had he lived to see it.

My mother came to my rescue. Reading the Evening News, she spotted a small advertisement describing a course at Napier Technical College. A course in a subject I'd never heard of: Interior Design. My meagre tally of qualifications met

Memory Spill

the entry requirements and my art portfolio impressed the interviewer, Mr Steel.

An architect had designed the modern college building with the ancient Merchison Tower as its central feature. This was the birthplace of John Napier who invented logarithms and made common the use of the decimal point in mathematics and arithmetic. Reading this in the course prospectus brought back the horrors of Secondary School. I had an involuntary spasm of anxiety as I recalled logarithm tables, slide rules and Mr Roberts's threepenny piece spinning through the chalk dust motes. But I needn't have worried, numerical skills were not essential. Maybe desirable but not essential. To my joy the government had celebrated my birthday that year by decimalising the currency and measurement. Overnight calculating the cost of a length of fabric became a lot easier. At my drawing board I would work using metres and millimetres, not inches, fractions of inches, feet and yards.

I arrived at the college on enrolment day and told to take the lift to the fifth floor. The lift was a moving series of open booths. I stepped into a booth as it clunked past and stepped out onto the fifth floor. I walked along the corridor and entered the classroom. A group of about fifteen students sat around while Mr Steel distributed enrolment paperwork. As I sat down at a desk I sensed the informality, so different from the discipline of school. Most of my fellow students were like me, local to Edinburgh with a few from other parts of Scotland and a few from other parts of the world. Harry Khan, with his Fu Manchu moustache was from Hong Kong or Taiwan and Sue was Indian but her family lived in Canada. We were the second intake, and the course had a pioneering freshness, the lecturers teaching us with energy and enthusiasm.

Freed from the oppressive atmosphere of school I was in a personal heaven. Art and design were the main subjects. Fred Carson taught art, drawing, painting, pottery and the history of architecture. Jimmy Steel who had interviewed me taught interior design and Mr Sanderson, the head of the department, painting and decorating techniques. A Dane, the Danish consul and local businessman, shared his experience with us and we attended a building technology class once a week. A massive Nigerian with a huge laugh taught ergonomics, something we had never heard of. Thanks to Jock Glass at Lasswade High School I was proficient in technical drawing, and my uncle Al, all these years ago in our sunlit lounge had taught me the principals of perspective. Both are the essential skills of interior design. Essential to convey your ideas to a client. It was a well-conceived course. Over the four years of the course there was less of the arty-farty stuff and more of the technical subjects. We were being trained to be employable as designers.

I had arrived dressed in what I considered the look of a fashionable designer. Influenced by Baxter Cooper the school art teacher I had a tweed jacket with leather elbow patches, cord trousers and suede shoes. I soon realised that this look suited a forty-year-old art teacher but was not the fashion statement of a teenage design student. Since nobody in authority seemed to care about students dress sense I hung my tweed jacket and cords in my wardrobe and attended college in my jeans, polo neck jersey and unique Great War leather flying coat, the latter substituted with an American bomber jacket in the warmth of spring and summer. I wore my dad's Royal Artillery tie as it had a trendy zigzag design until an RA veteran sat opposite me on a bus told me I was a disgrace.

To get us into the analytical mindset the first projects were designing polar expedition living spaces and spaceship interiors before progressing to more commercial environments: museums, offices and pubs. When completed our design schemes were displayed on the corridor wall and we were encouraged to criticise each others work. This resulted in bad tempered spats with students encased in thin skins sulking for days. We were being hardened for life outside college. Learning to take criticism on the chin.

Pub interiors we knew about. If there was a reason to celebrate we would head for one of the local pubs. Or if not to celebrate, to protest. At that time in Scotland the law banned women from bar areas of pubs and they were only allowed to drink in the lounge. One lunchtime in a show of solidarity with our sisters we mobbed the bar of a pub owned by Chick Murray, the famous comedian. The barman refused to serve us and after sitting around for ten minutes before we sheepishly left. A pointless protest without the publicity of a news headline. Occasionally the celebrations would get out of hand. One day we return to an afternoon class more than tipsy to find Fred Carson drumming his fingers on his desk. He told us we had to complete an important assessment project within two hours. Startled, we tried to think of ideas and concepts for the design some hypothetical interior and draw the plans and perspectives. At the end of class Fred gathered the work in then dumped our drunken daubs and scrawls in the waste bin and laughed as we filed out of the room to go to the next class.

On my eighteenth birthday the celebrations were excessive. I had acquired a taste for vodka and orange at the time and everyone at the impromptu lunchtime party bought me one. Fifteen students: fifteen vodka and orange shots. I got very drunk. We decided not to, or just forgot to go back to college. Instead someone suggested we go to the Odeon on Lothian Road to see 'The Magic Christian' a film starring Peter Sellars and improbably, Ringo Starr. On the way we called into a baker shop to get cream buns. It was here I had a memorable out-of-body experience. While my body stood unsteadily at the counter my mind soared to the ceiling and looked down as the shop assistant placed my chocolate éclair

Memory Spill

in a paper bag. Things didn't improve. As we sat slumped in the cinema, the film at the end of the bright cone of light began back to front with the end credits spooling in front of us. Annoying if you sober but disconcerting if you are stocious.

After watching the film in its correct sequence, we dispersed at the cinema steps and I headed to where I thought I had left my Morris Minor van. I must have found it since I had no recollection of the journey home. I woke up in bed where my mother had put me. It was about six o'clock and I could hear my dad coming in the front door. After going through the process of wondering where I was, then realising that I was in my bedroom I went downstairs. At the tea table my dad asked me about what I'd been up to at college. Mum looked across the table and smiled knowingly as I told a whopping lie.

The bus journey to and from college took for ever so dad had bought me the van. Even before I left school, my dad taught me to drive. He would take me out on quiet country roads near the village of Carrington. His car was a Vauxhall Velox, black with a bulbous body he had bought from the parents of his friend Keith Moncrieff. Modelled on the much larger American cars it had a bench seat with the gear shift mounted on the steering wheel and the handbrake down by the right leg. All straightforward unless your dad arranges for you to sit the test in a Ford Anglia with a floor mounted gear stick and the handbrake between the front seats. My first test was a comical catastrophe my hands searching for the gear stick on the steering wheel and the handbrake down by my leg. But I passed the test at the second attempt.

The van my father bought me was a Morris Minor. He knew a local man who was a GPO mechanic and reconditioning and selling the obsolete GPO vans was a side line. Cars, fuel and crucially insurance was cheap then. Most of my friends had old bangers too and where, in childhood and early adolescence we cycled everywhere, we now drove. At college I was the only one who had transport, and I was called on to run people around.

The second Christmas we were together a college friend Jimmy Thompson suggested distributing food to the needy. The catalyst was that he lived with a member of the Rankin family who owned a chain of fruit and vegetable stores in Edinburgh and happy to donate stuff from their business: vegetables, fruit and canned food. We continued gathering food donations from staff and students at the college while we found someone to tell us who in the needy in the community. A local minister or priest provided a list and one bitterly cold night we loaded my van with boxes.

Two cases stuck in my mind. One address was up a close, or passageway off the Royal Mile. We carried the box up a series of steps and knocked on a door. It swung open and a frail old lady stood before us. After explaining why we were there, she invited us into a room sparsely furnished with a bed and an armchair in front of a single bar electric fire. There was an open fireplace with a pile of ash like a miniature pit slag heap spilling out onto the floor that a cat had been using as a litter. In this cold, dirty room that smelt of cat piss a line of brass ornaments stood on the mantelpiece. These ornaments and the brass bed ends were as polished as any in a stately home. But no maids or footmen polished the old lady's brass. And the oddest thing: she was blind.

The other memorable recipient of our charity lived a few streets from the college. This lady lived in a room on the ground floor of Victorian town house. The room was high ceilinged with tall sash windows. It must have been a bugger to heat in winter. She was ancient, and tiny. Birdlike in the vast room. As we sat on her bed chatting we looked at the framed photographs that adorned the damp walls and arranged on the dressing table. Photographs of her in a tutu posing beside various handsome men with swept back oiled hair and wearing very tight tights that appeared to have selection of Rankin's fruit and veg stuffed down the front. Having someone to talk to pleased her. "This is me with Mikhail Baryshnikov...a wonderful dancer.... of course, I was a lot younger in those days...and, here, look, Rudolf...such a darling..."

As we walked along the pavement, I turned to wave to the ghostly figure in the window. She wouldn't see Rudolf this Christmas. Or Prancer or any of Santa's reindeer I thought. We drove away in a sorrowful silence thinking of the lonely old ballet dancer and the blind brass polisher.

We were now in the second year of the course. The three-year experiment with keeping the clocks fixed on Summertime throughout the year had begun. The people in London didn't notice much difference, but we did. At 10.00 in the morning we sat in our fifth-floor classroom watching the sun rise over the city. We were at the halfway point in the course. To progress to the third year of the course, we had to pass the intermediate exams. To succeed, we had to produce satisfactory work during the year then complete specific projects for assessment. It was a tough year, but we had the distraction of a foreign trip. A visit to York

For this visit to England we had T-shirts printed with a cartoon of Mickey Mouse wielding an axe and the slogan 'Ya Bass' thought to mean 'You bastard', but it is said to be from the Gaelic battle cry 'Aigh bas' meaning 'battle and die'. In the 1960s it had been adopted by the uber violent gang, The Glasgow Tongs who would chant 'Tongs Ya Bass!" prior to assaulting someone. The Tongs were the reason everyone avoided visiting Glasgow. Even the Triad and the Mafia gave Glasgow a wide berth. We thought all this a laugh but had the residents of York known the origin of the slogan we would have been stopped and searched at the city walls. But they let us in and we spent a week visiting the Minster, walking the walls, admiring Clifford's Tower and getting drunk in the evenings.

Memory Spill

After the intensity of the second year, the following year was uneventful, at least in the academic sense. But a student arriving from Huddersfield, England caused a stir. His father, a university lecturer, had moved to Edinburgh with his family. His son, halfway through an interior design course in England came with him. 'Hudders' as we Christened him was a serious student. We, after the traumas of the Intermediate Exams were not. Where Hudders seemed devoid of a sense of humour we enjoyed a laugh. As winter approached we sensed an opportunity for a practical joke.

We prepared the ground by talking up how bad winters in Scotland were, how deep the snow could be and how we students had to give up a week of our time to clear the pavements of snow. Hudders believed all this. He had received a letter from the Town Council advising him of the snow clearing station to report to and date he had to pick up his shovel. It looked authentic because we had typed the letter on a council letterhead procured by a friend of one of the class. Like his son Hudders father lacked a sense of humour and failed to sense that his son was having his leg pulled. Outraged that his son was to spend a vital week of his studies snow clearing he wrote to the Education Department demanding that his son be exempt from this onerous task. The Education department also suffering from a sense of humour bypass instigated a formal investigation. But faced with a wall of silence the investigation, like the light drizzle of snow that fell that year, melted away. We laugh ourselves silly behind our hands.

The intensity ratchet turned a few more notches in the fourth year. Failure meant four years of learning and our lives would slide down the pan and disappear round the U bend. During the final term we worked all day and into the night to complete our projects. These were not only for assessment by the examination board but would form the portfolio we would show

164

to prospective employers. The projects covered a wide range of design stuff: interior design to furniture design and appreciation of architecture to arts and crafts. For my interior design submission, I redesigned my dad's bank. Despite his misgivings about creating plans that would help bank robbers I persuaded my dad to let me survey his bank down near the docks at Granton. My furniture design project was a small desk I built in the cavernous workshop on the ground floor of the college and for Appreciation of Architecture I presented a comparison of my two favourite architects Corbusier and Frank Lloyd Wright. The finale of the year was an exhausting fortnight of exams. Written papers examined our knowledge of various aspects of design and business and the design projects tested our ability to produce interior design concepts within tight time constraints. The reward for success was to become an Associate of the British Institute of Interior Design and use the letters AIIBD after our names. There was also the Edmund Hudson Quaich, a traditional Scottish silver cup, for the designer of the year and a book token for best designer of my course. As I didn't think I deserved either I was truly shocked to win both. I had to attend an award ceremony and for the first time since my underwhelming piano performance in the church hall Bonnyrigg I clumped up the steps of to cross a stage. This time, not to sit at a piano but to be handed a silver cup by the wife of one of Edinburgh's construction magnates. My parents, sat on the front row, looked happier than after listening to my calamitous piano playing.

After a night of celebration with my friends at the University Student Union I had agreed to drop a student off at the halls of residence. I had no idea who Hamish was or how he came to be in my car. In fact, I was unsure about almost everything. I somehow knew he played rugby and that he was from Jedburgh in the borders where rugby is almost a religion.

Despite my friend's best efforts to subdue our passenger, Hamish amused himself shouting abuse and gesticulating at the drunks and policemen. Not a problem when on the move but I had to stop at the traffic lights where Blair Street crossed the Royal Mile into Cockburn Street. This was a spot busy with tourists during the day, but on tonight busy with drunks and policemen. A drunken lout taking exception to Hamish's antics staggered across the street tried to wrench open my door while the eighteen-stone prop forward from Jedburgh attempted to get out of the car to confront the drunk. I now had a Morris Minor two door saloon, the GPO van having fallen apart. The only way to exit from the rear of the car was to fold the driver's seat forward; difficult while the driver still sat in it. Hamish didn't see this as a problem. So, while the traffic lights remained red my head was being pounded against the windscreen while the steering wheel crushed the air from my lungs as Hamish used his rugby skills to force his way out of the car. Outside, the drunk had given up trying to open the door and expressed his frustration by kicking it Kung Fu style. With my face squashed against the glass I could see out of the corner of my eye two policemen about to join the fray. This was a worrying development. I had doubts I would be as successful with a breathalyser test as I had been with the college exams. To my relief the police grabbed Bruce McLee and Hamish slumped back into his seat. Then as the long arm of the law was about to tap on my window the lights turned to green and I screeched across the Royal mile and disappeared down Cockburn Street.

My dad joined me the next morning as I surveyed the damaged door, contemplating a visit to the local scrap yard where I would try and unbolt a door from a Morris Minor balanced on top of a stack of four other wrecks. "A good night out was it?" Then the dreaded question. "How's the job hunting going?"

When not laboriously writing application letters I had been cold calling on the architectural practices in the region hoping an architect with time on his hands would take pity, look through my portfolio of college work, and offer me a job. But the 1970s were just around the corner and optimism and employment were thin on the ground in equal measure. Then one night I met up with a college friend for a drink. He suggested trying some of the large furniture stores who might need the services of an interior designer.

I started with one of the biggest, Robert Frost and Sons in Shandwick Place known as just Frosts. Wearing the smart suit bought for the prize giving ceremony I manhandle my portfolio through the elegant polished hardwood doors, wiped my feet on the mat and asked a vigilant sale assistant if I could speak to the manager. I followed him as he sashayed through the displays of colourful fabrics to arrive at an office door with two seats against the wall.

"Please wait here and the manager will see you shortly." He said in an unctuous tone.

I sat and waited, inhaling the smell of furniture polish, carpet fibre and curtain fabrics while I rehearsed my pitch. Then the door squeaked opened and a small portly man appeared with a military bearing, a generous moustache and a shiny bald head.

"Good morning." He said, then with a sense of urgency commanded me to follow him as he set off at a quick pace and vanished into the forest of colourful fabric displays. Hindered by my portfolio, which I could just carry under my arm, I walked after him hunched over like Quasimodo. I emerged into a clearing in front of a lift where I found the small man waiting, his eyes silently tut-tutting. We ascended several floors, the creaking of the cables and hum of the lift motor the only sounds. The lift stopped, the door slid open and I followed the small man into the landing. He tapped on a door.

"Enter! said a voice from the other side.

Memory Spill

The small man opened the door, and I followed him into a spacious wood panelled boardroom. Three men, probably in their late thirties or early forties, sat at the far end of a table the size of a small aircraft carrier.

"This is Mr... em...em...." The small man was flustered.

"Wilson." I said helpfully.

"Em...yes. Mr Wilson."

As one of the men at the table searched through a pile of papers, I realised I was an unexpected guest at the party. When I had walked into the store as a speculative job seeker I had been confused for an invited candidate for an actual job interview.

The man at the stern of the aircraft carrier stopped pointlessly leafing through the pile of application letters and looked up at me. One thing Robert Frost and Sons valued above all else were good manners.

"Do please take a seat Mr Wilson."

I sat down, and the small man left the room, and in the manner of a butler, turned to close the door.

The three sons of Robert Frost introduced themselves and I began my impromptu interview for the position of apprentice salesman. They were impressed by my qualifications, the black and white photograph of me being presented with the Edmund Hudson Quaich and by the contents of my portfolio which I spread out across the table top. Then, after answering a lot of questions and asking a few, the trio exchanged looks and asked me to wait in the corridor outside. Leaving the room, I propped my portfolio against a cast iron radiator and sat down on a chair and listened to the muffled conversation in the boardroom and the occasional hum of the lift motor.

The door opened and the eldest of the siblings asked me to come back into the room. I had graduated from unemployed former student to apprentice salesman was mine. It wasn't what I wanted to do after four years studying Interior Design but as I was short of any other offers and short of cash I accepted. Robert Frost junior shook my hand and told me I was to report on the following Monday to Mr Tice, the head of the curtains department where I would start my apprenticeship.

I arrived home from my interview to find my mother at the dining room table wrapping raffia around a wire lampshade frame: she and my retired father had taken up a wide range of hobbies. Mum was into arts and crafts while dad was fermenting a deadly range of potent wines.

"Och, Well, that's grand Sandy," she said ramming the lampshade's plastic connector into the neck of a wine bottle. Then sensing my lack of enthusiasm. "At least it a job, son"

She was obviously thinking at least I would cease being a drain on their finances, depleted since my dad's retirement.   "Where's that going?" I asked looking at the garish pink lampshade sprouting from the neck of the dark green wine bottle.

"Your bedroom."

It wasn't exactly my bedroom. Since moving to this house, I shared a small bedroom with my elder brother. My parents were obviously not expecting both of us to impose on their hospitality for too long. Willie had left the agricultural college the year before and was a sales representative for a fertiliser company. The position came with a company car and a four-drawer filing cabinet. The car stood on the driveway and the cabinet stood between our two beds; a sort of high level bedside cabinet. My mother's arts and crafts bottle lamp would stand on top of the cabinet.

On the Sunday night I had the bedroom to myself. I closed my book intending to get a good night's sleep before starting my new job in the morning. I reached up to turn off my mother's hideous lamp high on the filing cabinet. The light switch clicked, and the room became dark as ink. In that brief instant I was aware that I was holding only the lampshade and that it had become detached from the bottle. I was just wondering where the bottle had gone when it hit me in the right eye with a meaty thud. In the morning as I carried out my ablutions I looked in the mirror. The face of an unsuccessful pugilist stared back. I thought, "For fu...!"

".... cks sake whit ye done tae yer face son." said my new boss. A small dapper man in his late fifties with wavy grey hair Mr Tice had an alter ego. I later discovered that when a customer appeared in front of him, he would slip into an obsequious voice and servile manner but when in front of his staff his use of language was so colourful it spanned the full chromatic spectrum of a rainbow.

I explained the unlikely story of my mother's home-made lamp which sounded so farfetched it was almost believable. But I could tell by the raised eyebrows he was hearing a 'Walked into the door' tale.

"Well, if I were you I'd get yer mum one o' those rugs making kits." He advised drily.

Before the store opened for business Mr Tice introduced me to my fellow members of staff who had just walked into the department: Mr Lowe and Mrs Alsop. Ernest was a tall fleshy man with a bald head and a genial disposition. He favoured loose fitting baggy clothes a fashion style I had seen in old black and white photos of my dad taken in the 1930s. Betty was a cheerful woman but if you didn't know her you might assume her to be a prim member of the Free Kirk. She wasn't. Betty was a laugh.

"Aye, well ye cannae face customers lookin' like that" said Mr Tice. I followed him down to the basement and he

Memory Spill

gave me a sort of stock taking task, probably fictitious, to hide me away.

Two days later with my eye a muted shade of yellow I emerged from the bowels of the store and allowed to face the customers. At my surprise interview the one thing that the directors failed to ask about was my arithmetical ability. At college I concealed this black hole in my education; slouched over a drawing board I had time to laborious do any necessary calculations, but standing in front of a customer while working out the drop and fullness of curtains was daunting. Once the length of the fabric had been calculated a bolt of the chosen fabric would be brought up from the basement.

I had watched Mr Tice emerge from the basement and cross the shop floor carrying a bolt of fabric and throw it onto the counter, like a wrestler slamming an opponent onto the canvas, then roll it out across the table and measure the required length. A pair of scissors would appear in his hand which he would spin like a cowboy's revolver before making a small nick in the fabric. He would then deftly slide the scissors across the fabric with a soft hiss to slice the cloth in a straight line. When I tried this in front of a customer the fabric would, to my mute horror, ruck up to produce a jagged edge. So, even if I had calculated the correct length the piece would invariably end up in the remnants pile. Even the wrapping up the fabric was a consummate performance. Brown paper would be creased and folded with origami exactness and string tied with knots that would have qualified for a Boy Scout badge. Mr Tice was an artiste, a magician of his trade: Mr Tice was David Nixon I was more Tommy Cooper.

Large, deep drawers beneath the counter held the scissors, measuring tapes, chalk and other tools of the department. When the process of wrapping the fabric the simplest way to close a drawer was to thrust it shut with your thighs. One day I watched from the counter opposite as Mr Lowe completed a sale. He dropped the scissors and ball of string into the drawer. As pushed it closed his polite expression of gratitude to the customer turned into a whimper, a low moan and his face turned a reddish purple. I thought he might have been have a heart attack. So too did Mr Tice who rushed over, grasped him by the elbow and led him through to the partitioned area behind the counter. I assured the concerned customer that Ernest would be fine. Betty, who was showing another customer a sample book looked across and swivelled her eyes toward the enclosed work area telling me to find out what was going on. So, I did.

Ernest was slumped in a chair with his hand between his legs still moaning while Mr Tice lent against the partition looking on with his hands on his knees. He was stifling a laugh as though someone had just told him a terrific joke. He looked up as I walked in.

"What's up?" I said taking in the strange scene.

"It's Ernest... Ernest.... he's...he's trapped his cock in one o' yon drawers...." he spluttered, stifling his laughter. I winced feeling the pain. Ernest had firmly pushed the counter drawer closed with his thighs and this action combined with his penchant for the looser Oxford Bags style of trouser and complementary loose-fitting underwear, had resulted in the painful and embarrassing injury.

As I walked out of the storage enclosure Betty's face appeared from behind one of the curtain fabric displays.

"What's up with Ernest?" She asked in a stage whisper.

Embarrassed, I self-consciously mimicked the injury and Betty's mouth became a pursed round circle. "Ooooh! Is he all right?" "I think so." I said uncertainly although I was feeling a bit queasy myself.

"He won't be feeling cocky for a while, then." Said Betty as she disappeared giggling into the forest of fabric display stands.

Memory Spill

Robert Frost and Sons was a retail business from a bygone age. David Croft probably visited Frosts on a holiday in Edinburgh and thought of the idea for the BBC comedy series 'Are You Being Served'.

One day a young professional couple oozing new money came into the department and selected curtains and blinds for the house they had just bought. It would have been a substantial sale. But, they wanted, expected a discount. Mr Tice was having a day off, so I went to seek the advice of the store manager with the moustache and shiny domed head. At the word discount he blanched. "Discount? This is Frosts! We do not offer discounts. If one offers discounts, every customer will ask for discounts. Then where will we be?"

"Profitable, I thought as I left his office to break the news to my bemused customers.

A week later a gaunt tall man dressed in a tweed suit marched through our department towards the entrance doors. The carpet department apprentice escorting the man stepped forward to hold open the door and gave a slight bow as the gentleman left the store. The customer was some Lord from some island off the west coast. Later that day Mr Tice leant conspiratorially on the counter beside me. "Y'ken that Laird. He's bought a wee Persian rug and because he's a laird, they're sending a van and twa men a' the way up to Skye and back. But they'll no give yon customer o' yours a discount. No way tae run a business these days."

The upper-class nature of the clientele was probably part of the reason that the apprentices had been, like the Brothers Frost, educated at Melville College, one of the Edinburgh public schools. The other apprentices could socially connect; I couldn't. As a product of a comprehensive and four years at a Technical College I had a socialist mind set. I refused to address customers as 'Sir' or 'Madam' and struggled with the plummy accents. One day a couple placed an order, and the paperwork required an address.

"Where?"

"Gellaine."

"Could you spell that, please?" I asked after several failed attempts to understand.

"Gellaine!" The lady said in the sort of voice you use when speak to foreigners.

"On the coast near North Berwick!"

I realise then she lived in Gullane which I had always assumed, as it was by the seaside, was pronounced the same as the 'gull' in seagull. It is much the same in Yorkshire where I now live. The stately home Harewood House is Harwood House to those of the higher echelons of society. But for the rest of us a hare is a hare not a har.

A few days before Christmas the floor manager asked us to stay late. I asked Mr Tice what it was all about. "Och, it happens every Christmas. It's a waste o' fuckin' time but y'll hae a laugh."

And it was a laugh. We all stood beside our respective counters as the ancient stooped figure of Mr Frost senior flanked by his sons shuffled passed. He waved his walking stick in the air croaking, "jolly good show, well done!" It was a 'Grace Bros' comedy moment.

Our department was the first stop in Mr Frosts tour of the shop. As the cortège disappeared into the carpet department Mr Tice nudged me.   "Thank the Lord that's ower. Let's get away home, son."

After Christmas I decided a career in a retail mausoleum was not for me. I applied for and got a job in Leeds with the John Collier Tailoring Group. Not on a shop floor but in the Architect's department designing shops. I think my resignation letter was accepted with relief; I was a failed

Memory Spill

experiment. One lunch time during my last week after a heavy night out with my college friends I retired to the furniture department and fell asleep in a comfy chair. I came around to hear voices approaching. It was the furniture sales apprentice with a customer. Too late to do anything I kept my eyes closed as the amused customer made a joke about 'sleeping on the job' and the apprentice muttered "how awfully sorry he was." On my way down the stairs the apprentice confronted me. He told me I was a disgrace and that he would jolly well report me. I told him I was leaving on Friday.

That Friday as I left the store I turned to look back at the shop front and the new discount store next door. Then behind me there was a dull clunk. I turned around to see a man standing outside the discount store with a can of emulsion paint at his feet, the handle in his hand and a splash of turquoise paint covering his shoes and his left leg of his flared trousers up to the knee. He cursed, then turned.

"See that pal." He said. "Cheap shite. They dinnae make things right nowadays."

Yes, I thought: as Bob Dylan had sung "Times they are a-changin'"

It was the start of the decade that would bring power cuts, strikes, three-day weeks and cheap shite. Frost and sons, purveyors of quality furniture, would face an uncertain future.

Memory Spill

Chapter 15
Closure

One day, when I was a student driving through Corstorphine I realised I wasn't far from my first childhood home. Curious to see how it had changed I made a detour and pulled up at the kerb side in my Morris 1000 ex GPO van.

To my astonishment, the house hadn't changed at all. It turned out that the lady who had bought the house from my parents inconveniently died before moving in and without making a will.

I opened the garden gate and walked into a world that had stood still for 13 years. The roof of the air raid shelter had collapsed and the scorch marks from the bunker fire had faded, but not much else had changed. As I looked through

Memory Spill

the filthy windows, I saw that the wallpaper was the same as when I was five years old. Memories washed over me; Andy Pandy, Watch with Mother, the din of the pots and pans being beaten by Mrs Williams, the smell of the damp earth of the air raid shelter and the charred wood of the coal bunker. I watched as the ghost of a small child, chased by cloud shadows flitted past me and through the back door into my first childhood home.

Almost at the same time the lights of another house of ghosts were dimming and about to go out. In my sixteenth-year Aunty Jen died. Unmarked by the Great War, she had been the life and soul of the house in Lasswade. She was buried in the graveyard across the road from the Primary School where the undertaker handed cards with a diagram of a coffin edged with numbers to the mourners massed at the cemetery entrance. My brother and I had been allocated ropes.

To the harsh grating call of the carrion crows in the woods, we strained on the ropes. As the rough hemp slid through my hands, I remembered Aunty Jen's stories, made us laugh and comforted us when we cried. She would have made a wonderful mother. Then as the coffin disappeared, Willie's feet scrabbled for purchase in the loose soil as he almost joined Jen in the hole. I was sure I could hear her laughing. She had been a muckle woman in personality, and in body. With the death of Aunty Jen, my granny and her brother sold the house and moved into a residential caravan on the new Kevockvale Caravan Park build in the grounds of the paper mill owner's house.

The contents of the house, my grand-grandfather's treasure trove, were sold by Harry to a sharp antiques dealer from the Grassmarket in Edinburgh. Anything that the dealer didn't buy or that wouldn't fit into the residential caravan, Harry burned in the back garden. During the upheaval of the move I came across a box of small photographs of Uncle Harry on holiday. We knew Harry would spend vacations on his own, often at hotels owned by the group he held shares in. The black and white snaps showed Harry standing in sunshine with groups of men or sitting with individual men on a hotel patio. The pictures scenes had a sense of intimacy, my uncle looking relaxed and happy. I placed the photos back in the box and closed the lid on my Uncle's sad secret life.

In my final walk through the empty house, through this time capsule, I wondered at the kitchen with the bath against the wall, at the rooms empty of the furniture of life, the sad squares and rectangles on the drawing room walls, evidence of the missing pictures. Then, for the first time I entered the workshop to the side of the main house. The door creaked open and sunlight flooded in to illuminate worktops covered with paint pots, brushes and other tools of the decorating trade. Almost as if the workmen had just finished for the day; a landlocked Marie Celeste.

The school too had changed hands. A developer bought the austere building to convert into residential flats. The new occupants would have stunning views over the Esk valley now unblemished by the paper mill with its tall chimney and with clean sweet water running in the river. Some residents would look out onto the graveyard, Michael Bannerman's gravestone no longer lonely in the far corner. But would the owners of the flats smell the chalk dust, hear the faint ghostly screams and laughter of children in the playground and the sharp slap of the tawes? Would they hear an American music teacher playing the upright piano as small voices sang of the buzzing bees in peppermint trees and big rock candy mountains?

With the sale and subsequent modernisation of my granny's house it became, along with the school, the paper mill and the post office just another faded memory of the village as it metamorphosed from a vibrant close-knit working community into a commuter hub of Edinburgh.

Another shade from my past appeared. I had a friend at Primary School who emigrated with his family to America. We had sat in the Lea Field opposite the church, two ten-year-olds, discussing this momentous event; what life would be like in USA, how different schools would be. Then eight years later he visited his home town and knocked on my door. I opened the door to a stranger. Stuart, a tanned muscular American GI with a buzz cut faced me, a pasty faced Scottish student with long hair. He had been fighting in Vietnam. Our life experiences poles apart, we didn't have much to share and I remember it being an uncomfortable reunion. I thought later of how if my grandfather had not died in the First World War my family would have emigrated to America. But, I thought too, that my mum wouldn't have met my dad and I would never have existed. We are all products of such twists of fate.

Not long after, we moved out of the house in Bonnyrigg. My dad, when he retired, sold our home, and we moved to a bungalow he had had built in Gorebridge. At the time of the move Willie and I had gone off on a holiday to Italy and I missed the chance to make a farewell tour of our home, my House of Memories. Decades later I would recall my childhood in a letter to my mother. My bonzer mum.

Chapter 16
My Bonzer Mum

When my father died, my mother proved incapable of living on her own, the sorrow, the sudden unexpected loneliness crushing her. Left to her own devices in Roslin, near Edinburgh, she stalked her GP, Dr Pope, phoning him at five in the morning with imagined ailments. Dr Pope, desperate for a quiet life, contacted me, pleading I do something. That something turned out to be moving her to Leeds where she lived with us for almost six years until her death. After a difficult transitional period, things settled down and mum conformed to our lifestyle. She learned to enjoy football, understanding the offside rule, but confused by action replays: "Och, is that not another goal!" Her limited range of cuisine expanded, from omelettes and dishes gleaned from a bizarre book called '100 dishes to make with mince', to encompass and enjoy Chinese takeaways, Indian curries and Italian pizzas. She read racy novels, red top newspapers and became a devotee of Coronation Street. Near the end of this period, and, close to the end of her life, I wrote her a letter. A Mother's Day letter.

Memory Spill

Like many families, my dad did all the interesting things with my older brother and me; took us on camping trips, bought the exciting fireworks and taught us swim and to drive. Our mother, to her two sons, was relatively uninteresting, but in reality, she was an essential support system. An unsung hero. Mum fed and clothed us, healed wounds, dried tears and cheered us on at sports days.

My letter was one of belated thanks and celebrated her life as a mother. I wrote it on impulse when I was working on a site in London, the Saturday before Mothering Sunday.

The letter told of the care she had taken of us as children. The things she made: Davy Crockett hats, my toy dog 'Smuff' that she had knitted for me and the fancy-dress costumes for Halloween. How she had inspired my lifelong love of books. I wrote of the freedom she allowed my older brother and me, in our childhood and adolescence, to take risks, enjoy ourselves, have fun. I recalled the summer evening in the garden when I was swatting the midges swirling around our heads; she stopped my killing spree and told me that each midge was a living being and that they didn't live a long life. Of how she told me that swallows, flying high, were a portent of good weather. I spoke of her enthusiasm for gardening, passed to my brother Willie, inspiring his career in Horticulture and how she stimulated my interest in Art, leading to a career as an interior designer.

Memory Spill

I thanked her for her support during the dark times of my late wife, Ann's, illness and death. And, I assured her, with honesty that Val and I and our children, had enjoyed having her live with us. Enriched our lives despite the initial, sometimes fraught, upheaval to our home.

With the letter finished, I needed to print it. So, I wandered down the street, to a shop offering printing, copying and secretarial services. A young, blond haired girl was about to lock the door.

"G'day," she replied when I said hello.

Then, in the 1990s, every receptionist and shop worker in London seemed to be an Aussie.

"I see you're about to close, but could you print this?" I asked.

She looked at her wristwatch, then back at me. "No drama, come on in," she said smiling.

I handed her the floppy disc, and she sat behind her desk and slid it into the hard drive.

"I'll just give it the once over," she said, as the letter appeared on her monitor.

She seemed to give it more than the once over. Irked that this 'Sheila' was reading my private letter, I was about to say something, but stopped myself as I realised a tear was rolling down her cheek.

"Strewth! I shouldn't be reading this, but what a dinkum letter," she said, "what a bloody bonzer mum you have!"

"She is," I agreed. "She's certainly that. Most mothers are, yours too I expect."

"I've not been back to my home, in Adelaide, to see my mum, for two years," she told me, in a sad voice. "I miss her, she's bonzer too."

Memory Spill

"Send her an email," I counselled. "I'm sure she's missing you just as much."

When I got home, I placed my letter in an envelope with a conventional card and left it, with a bouquet, on her bedside table. Later, that day, Mother's Day, I saw my mother, through her open bedroom door, almost for the first time in my life, quietly crying.

So, whenever I see swallows flying high, specks in the vast blue sky, or when I help a trapped small insect to escape from our home, help it enjoy the rest of its short life, she walks smiling into my mind. My bonzer mum.

Not long after my mother died, and I found memoirs she had written; her memories of Lasswade when she was a child in the decades after the First World War. I had the privilege to live when fragments of the post war village; the buildings, the social life and communal spirit she describes still existed. I have added her memoirs to my book. Mum would have loved that.

A time to remember

Ellen E Wilson

When one has reached and passed the half—century in one's life-span it is time to remember and while memory is still clear, to put down on paper a record of the old days - the time of one's youth. So, let me take you on a tour of Lasswade as I knew the village when I was a child in the 1920s and 1930s.

Today the village is but a pale ghost of what it was then - a bustling community full of little houses and shops and peopled by many families busy, happy and contented folk. The main place of employment was Mr Todd's St Leonards Paper Mill whose lum (chimney) towered over the village though a few men folk worked as miners at Loanhead pit.

The people were not rich in money terms, but they were rich in friendship and in being part of a community that cared about the place where they lived and their neighbours. When there was a crisis or calamity there was always a hand stretched out to help, and if there was reason for celebration then the whole village rejoiced together.

Let us begin our journey near the foot of the Wee Brae. In Bras Cottage (underneath the Wee Brae Hall) lived Henry Young and his family. He was the Beadle of the United Free Church at the foot of the brae. Later it was known as Strathesk Church and now is Lasswade Parish Church.

Opposite the church were the business premises of Alexander Lothian & Sons Painters and Decorators which my grandfather had established in 1884; I was born in the house above the shop. Then at the corner of Eldin Place was the grocer's shop belonging to Mr Andrew Scott who had taken it over after the death of Jim McKay. Grocery deliveries in Mr McKay's day were made by pony and trap.

Along from Mr Scott's shop lived Mr Gray the tailor (where Esk Valley Camera Club now meets). The remainder of Eldin Place provided housing for several families - the McLeans, the Kirks, the Browns, the Campbells and others. Over the road at the top of the Steps was the Post Office and general store in the capable hands of Mr Billy Stewart and his wife. Mr Stewart served a term as Provost of Lasswade.

Next door to the Post Office (where the electric sub-station now stands) was the workshop of David Reid, carpenter, cabinet maker and funeral undertaker. He was my grandfather's close friend.

At the corner of Elm Row was the garage managed by Mr Baird and his son Joe (to be followed later by Mr David Burns and family). Across the road was the red sandstone building of the Parochial Board where the Parish Registrar, Mr James Robb, recorded the local Births, Deaths and Marriages. In the days before the Welfare State needy people went there for Parish Relief. Mr Robb was succeeded by Mr William Sked.

The Elm Row was full of little houses occupied mainly by workers at the paper mill or miners from the local pits. In a cottage in the middle of Elm Row lived Mrs MacIntosh, a kindly sweet faced, white haired lady. She was the village midwife, well thought of by our three doctors: Dr Robertson, Dr Chas Somerville and Dr John Young. Her presence was invaluable at the birth of a baby or when someone was suddenly struck down by serious illness or death.

Down from the Parochial Board lived Mrs Yorkston and her sister who on Saturday mornings ran a playgroup for the very young children. These ladies were great story tellers and there were vast heaps of picture books. Before going home each child was given a cup of milk and a slice of home-made seed cake. (Shall I ever forget that seed cake?) All this I may say was provided for the price of one old penny. Incidentally, one old penny took us into the matinee at Bonnyrigg Picture House on Saturday afternoons. The proprietor was Mr Readshaw and Miss Mary Currie from the village was employed there for several years as an usherette.

Next to the Yorkston house was a baby linen and haberdashery shop run by Miss Maggie Hardie; later when she died it was taken over by Mrs Hay. Long years before, this shop had been a baker's shop with the bake house below. Over the doorway there was an interesting carved stone plaque depicting sheaves of corn. When this building was demolished in the 1950s this stone, I believe was removed to the Museum of Antiquities in Edinburgh.

Further on down Elm Row was the sweet shop belonging to Mrs Hay's daughter Nettie. Then we come to the shop run by the Murdoch brother, a cobblers and shoe repairers. Candle Row was the lane at the back of these houses and ran almost parallel but at a lower level to Elm Row, at the point where it re-joined Elm Row was the shop owned by Mr James Henderson outfitter, clothier and general draper. Because of its shape this building was known locally as The Coffin House. Here too were more little houses.

Over the road from Coffin House was Mr Robert Arnot's plumber's business with his house above almost adjacent to Mr Johnny Black, Grocer & Italian Warehouseman whose emporium lay at the foot of the Post Office Steps. It was really something of a delicatessen store supplying such exotic merchandise as stuffed olives, maraschino cherries and pickled walnuts all beautifully displayed in rows of glass jars and stem ginger in decorated stone ginger jars. There were cheeses and wines from foreign parts. Much of Mr Black's custom came from the big houses in the Braeheads, Broomieknowe and the surrounding area, deliveries being made by pony and trap. The village folk of course could buy everyday commodities such as tea and sugar scooped out from big bins and weighed and packaged at the counter. The coffee was ground while you waited, and wedges of cheddar were cut as required from the whole cheese with a thin steel wire. Sides of bacon and smoked hams hung from the ceiling and canisters of herbs and spices lined the shelves. For a penny, we could buy sugar crystals on a string. The delicious aroma of that shop still lives with me after all these years.

It is hard to visualise them today but just up by the Post Office Steps from Black's shop several houses managed to fit themselves in. Euphemia Stebbings sweet shop was tucked in between Johnny Black's and Mr Kirk the butcher whose shop was at the corner of West Mill Road which led to the paper mill. Mr Kirk was often assisted in the shop by his wife. Both Mr and Mrs Kirk were very gifted musicians always in demand for concerts and other local functions. Facing them over the road was the building at Bridgend where Mr Fergus Stewart the chemist and Mr Bell the baker had their shops with two or three houses above them.

Returning to Coffin House and entering Candle Row with its numerous little houses we come to the workshop of our other carpenter Mr Peter Lockie. He lived with his wife and family in the cottage at the top left of Elm Row where the road hairpins to Bonnyrigg and known to everyone even to this day as Lockie's Corner; a fitting memorial to a very kindly man.

From Candle Row, we walk down past the War Memorial and the public park to Mrs Kelly's market garden at Middle Mills where a big basket of fresh vegetables would cost you about 2/- (10p).

Retracing our steps to Elm Row we cross the bridge over the North Esk and turn left into School Green with its line of trees and in between them the Loupin Stanes. On their way to and from school it was a favourite game of the children to leapfrog over these stones; the last stone in the row was rather tall and was classed as a 'henner'.

At the end of School Green was Tom Aitken's dairy. Before Tom the dairy had been run by Johnnie Beattie and his sister Jane; Johnnie Beattie was the first Provost of Lasswade. Mr Aitken grazed his cows either in the Cow Park below Eldin House (now Nazareth House) or in the Glebe up the Back Road past the Old Parish Kirk (now demolished).

Opposite the dairy, we find the church hall which was originally the Parish School of Lasswade. This was the centre of the village jollifications, concerts, dances and weddings. Next to it is the original schoolmaster's house then the Bank Buildings in the lower flat of which my Grandparents set up house after their marriage in 1884. 'The bank' was the local branch of the City of Glasgow Bank which went bust in 1878 and was subsequently converted into flats.

Next to the Bank Building was the telephone exchange and at the corner Mr Montgomerie's grocer's shop. Round into the High Street and tucked as it were into a corner was Mr Harry Royle's establishment reached by an elegant flight of

Memory Spill

steps with wrought iron railings. Purveyor of sweets, lemonade, cigarettes etc. and of 'real Italian ice cream' a pint jug of which for Sunday lunch could be purchased for 1/6 (7½p). I seem to remember he had a billiard saloon behind the shop.

Further along was the Foresters Arms (now The Laird and Dog) run by Mr and Mrs Jack whose son Lawson was a keen rugby player. Here too was the Gospel Wynd much used by villagers making their way to Kirk and cemetery. Next came Tom Whyte the blacksmith; his shop with its forge was of quaint architecture, very old with diamond paned windows. He supplied the villagers with all their DIY needs in the way of screws, nails, bolts and general ironmongery. His professional services were in constant demand by the local farms and estates.

When winter set in he also made skates. The skating and curling ponds were situated just beyond the gates to the manse drive in the Edinburgh Road; when the ice was bearing, the ponds at night were lit by oil lamps hung on poles and the curlers and skaters had a high old time.

Above the smiddy was the Police Station with the constable's house while across the road were two cottages, one occupied by Danny Munro the Parish Kirk beadle and the other by the Stirling family. Along from St Ann's House was the sweet shop run by wee Mrs Cousins, a small woman hut with a big heart where children were concerned. Her tiny shop was an Aladdin's cave of confectionery. I still remember her gold-rimmed spectacles and the little steel hammer she used to break up the large slabs of toffee.

Just here stands the Town Hall (now a small factory); in addition to political and council meetings it was much used for social functions, fancy dress balls and the local Unionist Association annual ball. In the open space between the Hall and the paper shop was a row of houses. In those days, the newsagent's shop was run by old Mrs Black to be followed by

190

Memory Spill

Mrs Meldrum and later by Mrs Clark. At the end of the block next to the bridge was Mr Stirling's general store.

Back to the School Brae; half way up at 'Sunnybrae' was Mr Forrest's market garden where he grew fruits of all kinds for the market. We, as schoolchildren spent many happy days there during the summer holidays berry picking at four pence per hour. There were tomato houses and a vinery.

At the top of the brae was our school - Lasswade Secondary School. It was a good school with a splendid band of teachers, dedicated men and women who seemed to stay with us right through our years at school. One or two of them were still there when my own children went to school. At secondary level pupils came from as far away as Penicuik, Polton, Roslin and Loanhead. In those days, there were no school dinners; the children carried 'lunch pieces'.

With very little motor traffic, we children could play quite safely in the streets. Two cars I can remember were SY-8 belonging to the Hoods of Midfield House and SY-10 belonging to Waldie of Polton both being local coal-owners. Occasionally one of the doctors would drive past on his rounds or the Rev R. H. Pryde the Parish Kirk minister who also owned a car. Until the SMT (Scottish Motor Traction) arrived with their bus service via Loanhead to Edinburgh the main link with the city was by rail from Lasswade station via

Memory Spill

Broomieknowe, Eskbank and Portobello.

Over and above the natural playground of the School Green and the public park, there was the vast space for adventure provided by the Braeheads, Kevock and the Haveril Woods. Children anywhere in those days were as safe as houses. We had a great respect for authority - the schoolmaster, the school Jannie, the ministers, the village bobby and even the scaffy who saw to it that we did not become litter louts. Many an ear was cuffed in the process. We had law and we had order. Palmies were dealt out at school when necessary which was not very often, and parents did not go calling for redress at judicial courts. In fact, we children found it prudent to keep quiet about the administration of the strap at school because if we complained at home we could end up with another lecture and "Ye shouldn't ha done that anyway".

So, we come to the end of a sentimental journey. It has been quite difficult for me to fill in so many vacant spaces with houses, shops and people. Came the day when Lasswade was joined to Bonnyrigg making one burgh and the village sank slowly into decline; from a self-sufficient bustling community Lasswade has become another dormitory of Edinburgh,

First the people were moved from the old village houses to the brand-new housing scheme in Dobbies Road; a good many of them were not keen to move and often said that if houses were built in Lasswade they would like to come back. Just before the war a small group of Swedish timber houses was built at Melville View.

The old village houses were left empty to rot and decay. One by one the shops and small businesses closed down for the customers were no longer there. In the 1950's the scene of devastation was such that one visitor enquired if we had suffered bomb damage in the war! The old Parish Kirk on the hill had to be demolished because of dry rot. Foreign competition ensured the demise of St Leonards Paper Mill; the lum (chimney) which had stood guard over the village for so many years was felled and the mill stripped and razed to the ground. However succeeding councils did their best to cover up the scars. The School Green was landscaped as well as other vacant spaces; trees, flowers and shrubs were planted, and the War Memorial rescued from years of neglect. But when you move the people from a village you rip the heart out of it. Lasswade will never be the same again but it still remains an attractive and pleasant place to live in. After all, Lasswade will always have its place in history.

Memory Spill

An Englishwoman in Lasswade

Ellen E Wilson

My Grandmother, Ellen Harris was born in Bicester, Oxfordshire in 1862. She was the daughter of Miss Harris, a maid in a country house near that town; In fact, my Grandmother was the offspring of a well-to-do man and his maid! The gentleman, whether from a real fondness for the girl he had seduced or from a feeling of obligation to the girl who was his illegitimate daughter made it plain to his family that he wished to honour that obligation, insisting upon providing for young Ellen's proper education. In consequence, she was provided for to the extent of a place being found for her in a private boarding school, and she was suitably set up sartorially. According to my Grandmother, she was all packed up ready to embark upon this new life when the gentleman died suddenly. His family did not cast her off as might have been expected. Instead they arranged for her to be settled in the household of friends who lived in a large country house near Bexley, Kent as under-nursemaid to their children. She would then have been fourteen years of age.

In the ensuing period of years, she progressed from the lowly state of nursemaid to become a well thought of and much-loved nanny to the family. Her employers were very well off and of some consequence, for the whole household down to the servants, the gardeners and the estate workers lived in some comfort. For instance, my Grandmother had at her disposal as the children's nanny a dogcart with a groom to drive her and the children around on shopping expeditions to the nearby town or just simply to 'take the air' in the beautiful countryside around the estate.

'Mi-Lady', as Granny called the Lady of the House, was very beautiful. Granny remembered 'Mi-Lady' favouring Pond's Face Cream and Pear's soap for the care of her complexion. There was a Lady's maid who took charge of 'Mi-Lady's' elegant gowns and clothes and a French hairdresser whose sole occupation was the care of Madame's hair.

At this time, my Grandmother would be in her 21st year and pretty enough for the French hairdresser to display romantic inclinations towards her. She was very petite, fair haired and blue eyed. They had been 'walking out' she and the Frenchman, for some time, when suddenly a tall well set up Scottish man arrived on the scene. He (my Grandfather-to-be) had been sent by his father (of Messrs Lothian & Kinross, Wallpaper Merchants of Edinburgh) to the School of Art in London to study Interior Design.

On this occasion, he had travelled down from London as assistant to a senior Art Designer from the School who was advising on the decoration of several rooms in the house at Bexley. The arrival of Alexander Lothian at Bexley put paid to the romance between the French hairdresser and Ellen the children's nanny. The handsome young man from Edinburgh

Memory Spill

swept my grandmother off her feet.

By the time Art School commission at Bexley was complete Alexander Lothian had proposed marriage to Ellen Harris and had been accepted; the wedding was to take place in Scotland, 'Her Ladyship' was quite enthralled with the whirlwind romance and set about arranging for the whole of the trousseau (six of everything!) and the wedding dress which was a marvellous gift. 'Mi-lady' and her husband also presented Ellen with a long gold chain and locket, and from the children who had been in her care, there was a gold brooch in the shape of a horse-shoe with the initials 'B H' engraved upon it. These two items are now in the possession of my cousin Jane. So, Ellen travelled to Edinburgh with her betrothed to be introduced to his family and to a very different way of life as the wife of Alexander Lothian, On 6th June 1884 they were married in the Lothian family home at 41 James Street, Pilrig, Edinburgh.

Having left the beautiful countryside of Kent Ellen Harris and her new husband Alexander Lothian set up house in the Bank Building in the little village of Lasswade, a far cry from the luxurious surroundings she had enjoyed in the country house near Bexley. In due course on 8th May 1885 my mother, Laura Ann was born in the house at Bank Buildings, but by the time the rest of their family arrived (Alexander John, William Graham, Harry Dickson and Jessie Alexandra) my Grandfather had bought the Decorating business with house above at Polton Road, Lasswade. He employed between 14 and 20 painters, journeymen and apprentices. The business flourished and as the years went by the services of Mr Lothian of Lasswade were much sought after by the folk who lived in the 'Big Houses' roundabout who required his expertise and advice on their interior decorating. He also had an eye for good watercolours and oil paintings, antique furniture and such like his advice on which was also sought by those people who were intent on investing in such things.

Memory Spill

The sitting room upstairs in my Grandparent's house was a world of wonders for me. I can see it yet in my mind's eye with all the wonderful paintings on the wall, the elegant polished mahogany table and chairs, the Chippendale and Sheraton side tables with the collection of polished brass candlesticks and the brass samovar. The corner cupboard held a collection of beautiful Crown Derby and Spode china along with some antique ornaments. The floor boasted a lovely old Brussels carpet and the curtains of heavy jade brocade were tied back with embroidered ties. The mantelpiece was unique in that it had been fashioned from part of a four-poster bed of carved mahogany. On the hearth, there were brightly polished brass fire irons and several large brightly coloured foreign sea shells. As children, my cousins and I were allowed to hold one of these shells carefully to our ears to 'hear the sea'. And we did hear the sea.

There was a good upright piano. When I was seven years old I was introduced to the intricacies of playing the instrument by Miss Muirhead of Broomieknowe; one hour's practice every day but never on a Sunday The Sabbath was a day of rest; the pattern always was the Church Service in the morning followed by Sunday School and the Church Service again in the evening. Granny worked unstintingly for the Church and my Grandfather was an Elder. After the family Sunday dinner Granny would retire to the room upstairs for what she called her forty winks. I remember when I was very small sitting quietly at her knee I would count very slowly in my head up to forty then wait hopefully for her to wake up and talk to me. When she did, she told me tales of her childhood in Kent. I listened enthralled to her descriptions of the leafy lanes, the meadows full of wild flowers and the wonderful floral displays in the gardens of the thatched cottages. In spring, there was the mossy dell where she and the other children gathered primroses and cowslips.

Early summer carpeted the woods near her home with

bluebells and soon the whole countryside was covered in a haze of pink and white apple, pear and plum blossom. Small wonder that Kent was known as the 'Garden of England' - and still is.

Autumn came, and everyone went picking blackberries for jam, crab apples for jelly and sloe berries which the cottagers made into sloe gin. Then the children plundered the woods and hedgerows gathering cobs, filberts and hazelnuts. The Great Meadow also yielded a harvest of mushrooms. Nothing in the countryside was ever wasted. During the summer too, many people were busily employed in the hop fields gathering hops ready for the brewers. The Harris family was engaged in market gardening near Wantage; probably that is why I inherited the passion for growing plants which has been with me all my life.

I can't remember Granny talking about her mother. I never found out about her or what happened to her, but she did talk at length about her Grandmother, Ann Cowley who could trace a slight connection far back with the writer and poet Abraham Cowley who as well as being a writer of some note in his day was a Government Agent in the reign of Charles II. I still have by me a leather-bound copy of the 'Works of Abraham Cowley' handed down in the family as a very precious possession.

At the time of these tales told by my Grandmother on Sunday afternoons she would be over 60 years old. In 1920 when he was 61 my Grandfather Alexander Lothian had died suddenly of a stroke. Three years earlier the family had suffered the loss of my Father, Clem Walter who was killed at the 3rd Battle of Arras on 9th April 1917. He had gone off to the war in the first flush of patriotism, leaving my Mother to return to her family home in Lasswade where I was born on 7 May 1915. These two blows must have shaken the family badly but as happens in the scheme of things people pick up the pieces and carry on. The Painting and Decorating business was taken over by Granny's second son William (my Uncle Bill).

When my Grandfather died, my Grandmother went into mourning and like Queen Victoria never came out of her 'widow's weeds'. I can't remember her ever wearing any other colour than black. I recollect strongly her deep love of her Grandmother; it was a reciprocal adoration, and like my Grandmother I was brought up by my Grandmother. She was a very gifted needlewoman and she taught me all I know about that craft, her fine sewing, feather-stitching and embroidery were exquisite. She was also adept at tatting; to my regret I was never able to master that art!

My Mother on her return to her old home applied herself to the household duties, the day to day chores for a fairly large family but Granny saw to all the cooking and baking. She never seemed to work with recipes; it was all in her head. She was an excellent cook providing good and nourishing meals for all her family. I shall never forget Christmas preparations in our house; the delicious tangy smell of orange and lemon peel and the sharp warm smell of rum and brandy when we gathered around to stir the plum pudding mixture for luck. What a busy household ours was! Hands were never idle.

The one complaint about me was that I always had my nose in a book. Reading books was looked upon askance by all the family except Granny. Books were my other great passion and she encouraged me to read all kinds of books and she bought me Arthur Mee's Children's Encyclopaedia for my seventh birthday. That certainly furthered my education! Granny was the one person in my life I was in terror of losing. I worried about that for some time after my Grandfather's death but as the years went by Granny seemed to go on forever and I stopped holding my breath. She never went back to Kent.

The Harris relations came north from time to time; Granny's nieces Nell and Kathy Harris and a nephew Harry

Memory Spill

Harris. Then we saw a lot of my Grandmother's cousin Auntie Laura (Harris) who was already in Edinburgh in charge of the kitchen in the house of the Younger family the well-known brewers. There, as was the custom of the time, she was referred to as 'Mrs' Harris holding quite an exalted position in the household. We all loved Auntie Laura and visited her often. She was such a jolly plump amusing person so full of wit and humour; she was a first rate cook and we looked forward to her coming to stay with us at Lasswade for a wee holiday. We often visited her in Edinburgh and enjoyed her really sumptuous teas in her vast kitchen while all her staff scurried about getting everything ready for the Family's meal 'upstairs'. My cousins and I were allowed to take turnabout standing on a chair to grind the coffee beans; that was the high point of the visit for us — that delicious aroma of freshly ground coffee beans!

Our house at Lasswade had an ever-open door. It would not be unusual for someone like Viscount Melville to wander in unannounced, through the shop, right into the kitchen even into the scullery looking for Granny or my Mother or my Grandfather whom His Lordship had really come to see. Then there were all the children going up and down to the school. All the cuts, bumps and bruises were brought to our door for immediate first aid by Granny. She never applied disinfectant or ointment; rather it was "We'll just anoint this with something to make it better". The bandaged casualty would then go away, tears dried and happy. She loved and cared about any children who came her way.

Granny also had frequent visits from people collecting for various good causes - The Grass Market Mission, The Salvation Army, The Red Cross, and The RNLI - they all received a donation. There was one lady who came without fail once a year collecting for 'The Boozers League'; in my childish innocence, I thought she was collecting for a handout of intoxicating beverages! Then there was Old Tage the tramp

Memory Spill

who called almost weekly. The look of the tall unkempt shambling man nearly scared the wits out of me, but he was harmless enough. Granny filled his old syrup tin with tea and sent him on his way with a large 'doorstep' of bread and jam. One winter he failed to appear, and we heard that he had been found dead in a secluded part of the Braeheads. I had always wondered why he walked so funny; it was discovered that he had hidden all his worldly wealth in his boots, winding hundreds of pounds in notes round and round with strips of old cloth like army puttees.

Granny never turned anyone away; help was always given when it was needed. In fact, it was the way of Lasswade folk; they always rallied around and helped each other when the necessity arose. There was no such thing as the Department of Health and Social Security, only the Parochial Board and Poor Relief and folk lived in fear of that happening to them especially when old and perhaps senile or 'wandered in the head' and being taken to Rosslynlee Asylum or the Poor House in Dalkeith.

When war broke out in 1939 Granny was the driving force where our family was concerned, and idle hands were frowned upon. Everyone got busy with knitting needles and wool making 'comforts for the troops'. We made quite a pile of navy socks, scarves, gloves and mittens to send to the men of HMS Edinburgh which not long afterwards was torpedoed while on convoy duty to Murmansk. Then we would switch to 'comforts' for the Army or the RAF; it was a busy, busy time.

By the time I was in uniform myself in the ATS serving away from home Granny had suffered a slight stroke, collapsing in Church one Sunday. A year or so later she suffered another massive stroke from which she never recovered, confined to bed, unable to move and in a coma. Her last words to me were: 'Remind them, Nell to order plenty of boiled ham for your wedding'. That must sound laughable, but village weddings were often held at home or in the village hall and the usual centrepiece of the Wedding Breakfast was a large boiled ham. Generally, everyone joined in, cooking and baking to provide a long, long table groaning with food and village weddings were certainly joyous occasions for everyone to enjoy until rationing and other wartime circumstances brought many changes to the old ways of doing things.

When Granny suffered her last illness, I was engaged to be married but because of the war it was over two years before my happy wedding day arrived. Sadly, she did not live to see that great day. She died on 21st September 1943 and I was given special leave from the Army to attend her funeral.

Ellen Harris was a small woman in stature, but she had a great big heart. The whole village grieved at her passing. I shall never forget her, a much loved and loving Granny whose memory lives on in my heart.

Memory Spill

The village cabinet maker

Ellen E Wilson

Davy Reid was my Grandfather's friend; they were very close, helping each other in many ways in the way of business. Davy was a tall man, spare of figure with a moustache that drooped, making him look a little sad until his face lit up with laughter and those deep blue eyes of his shone. His eyes always looked as if they were scanning far horizons. Indeed, they might have done so for as a young man he had gone to Canada to find his fortune, He did just that; building up a prosperous joinery business and I understand from my Grandparents, he had planned to marry out there and settle down. He returned to Scotland to tell his parents of his plans with the firm intention of persuading them to return to Canada with him. They refused. The wringing of hands began; who was going to look after them in their old age? What about his sister Lisbeth who was in 'delicate health' and unmarried? Davy had made his one big mistake. In the end, he was prevailed upon to give up his business in Canada and all his

Memory Spill

plans for a fine future there. He gave in, electing to stay in Scotland with his parents and sister.

By the time I was born in the house at Polton Road in the spring of 1915 Davy's old parents had long since died and he was left to look after his sister Lisbeth who seemed to be a chronic invalid, I can't ever remember seeing Lisbeth Reid; she was something of a recluse shutting herself away in their house (now gone) opposite Spring Bank. Davy continued to come about our house and shop opposite Strathesk Church at the foot of the Wee Bras and his friendship with my Grandfather Alick Lothian the Painter and Decorator became his one solace in life. They both enjoyed many happy hours of conviviality together until the dreadful night when my Grandfather died. He had been helping Davy with a 'chesting' and the effort of lifting a very heavy lady into her coffin was too much for him. He had collapsed across the coffin, dying of a heart attack and brain haemorrhage. When he brought my Grandfather's body home Davy was distraught. We were all distraught and weeping. Davy stood with tears streaming down his cheeks. It was the first time I had seen a grown man weep. I joined him in his misery for I too had lost my best friend. I was just four years old.

Davy was fond of children and my cousins and I often toddled down to his workshop which was situated where the electricity sub-station now stands at the Junction of Polton Road and Elm Row. With our teddy bears and dolls, we sat amongst the wood shavings bedecking our dolls' heads with the pinewood curls. Even now I have only to smell the scent of pinewood and I remember Davy. He always had time to put off with the bairns. In fact, he would have made a fine family man, and that was the pity of it all.

In the 1920s when we had not the lifesaving modern drugs, Death was a frequent visitor to the village. Older people passed away in the nature of things, but tuberculosis (TB) was the main scourge while diphtheria, whooping cough, measles, scarlet fever and pneumonia could be fatal to a child or a very young person. Consequently, a large part of his business was in the making of coffins, most of them for people he knew well. No trouble was spared in the fashioning of each coffin; every detail and embellishment was exact and beautiful. Sometimes when he had completed his work on a coffin he would lift us up to let us see his finished creation. We looked down in wonder on the lovely white sateen-padded interior; the soft lace edged pillow and the lace edging all-round the top of the coffin.

It was the last service he could render to those who had passed away, people he had known. He carried out his work with pride, and, I daresay with an unspoken prayer for the departed, He was a staunch Kirk man — a good and faithful servant to his God. The final decoration was the coffin plates. These were expertly lettered by hand by my Uncle Al or Uncle Bill on the scrubbed table in our kitchen. The wet painted lettering was sealed by a sprinkling of gold dust. Then my cousin Jane and I carried the coffin plate down to Davy's workshop, instructed to hold it well away from our frocks and not to smudge the paint. Very elegant, we thought, were the brass coffin plates which were used for the solid oak coffins. In a funny sort of way, we children got used to coffins and coffin plates from a very early age. We were not upset by any of it, looking on it as part of village life!

Then there were the funerals, carried out with meticulous formality; the big black hearse drawn by two fine black horses, and Davy seated beside the driver smartly turned out in his black top hat, frock coat and a black stock with a pearl tie pin Davy was a bit of a Don Quixote, occasionally 'tilting at windmills' One of his windmills was the Parish Kirk Minister who wanted Davy to arrange for the funerals to go up the steep School Brae instead of up the drive past the Gospel Wynd and the gate of the manse. The Lady of the Manse also was very insistent in regard to this arrangement. Davy objected to this in no uncertain terms and

Memory Spill

spoke his mind; he wouldn't have his horses drag a heavy hearse up the steep School Brae when the drive which passed the Manse was so much easier, His angry riposte to the Minister was reported by one onlooker: "if ye try tae stop the funerals gaun up by the Manse, Ah'll clure ye wi ma fore hammer". For a long time, as a mark of defiance Davy sat up beside the driver of the hearse with his fore hammer laid across his knees. The matter was not referred to again.

Davy never got over the death of my Grandfather. He came regularly to our house, just wandering in through the shop into the kitchen in the middle of the working day, then he would settle down to a wee crack with my Granny about the on-goings in the village. His sister was always something of a trial to him. Occasionally he would appear in our kitchen to announce: "Lisbeth has got the glooms!" After a chat and a gossip, he would wander over to The Foresters' Arms to drown his sorrows. Later he could be seen wending his erratic and unsteady way homewards up the Polton Road. Granny would take my cousins, Jane and Alick and me to the front door to witness at first hand "What strong drink does to a man". Small wonder that a few years later we joined the Band of Hope meeting in the Wee Brae Hall and signed the pledge!

Two of his visits to our house I remember vividly. Once after a visit to the Foresters' Arms, he arrived in our kitchen very unsteady on his feet and announced to the world at large: "I fear no foe in shining armour!" and before our astonished gaze lurched backwards from the kitchen into the scullery, ending up by sitting down in a tub of bed-linen soaking in cold water ready for the Monday wash. That sobered him up! Then we had to dry him out before he could go home to Lisbeth. On another memorable occasion, he arrived in our kitchen declaiming: "I have no fear of any mortal man" and sat down on top of our American range which had been stoked up to heat the flat irons for the ironing. Again, Granny came to the rescue, stitching a patch on the seat of his trousers with her sewing machine before he could go home in a decent condition.

And another tale of Davy was told to me by my family. Once, when my Grandfather was still alive, Davy had gone to the Musselburgh Races with rather a large sum of money from a customer in his pocket and his love of horses got the better of him. He became gloriously tipsy and bought a race-horse! Getting him out of that fix took a good deal of effort on the part of my Grandfather and Davy's lawyer. Later, when he had sobered up be was quite abashed at what he had done. I have a feeling that during his days in Canada he must have learned to ride and the sight of all these beautiful animals at the racecourse had been just too much.

By the time I had reached my late teenage years Lasswade was changing. One by one the families were moved out from their little houses and cottages and re-housed in the new Swedish timber houses or in the new Council houses at Dobbies Road. Davy had retired, giving up his business to look after Lisbeth; where his workshop had been The Lothian's Electric Power Company had built the sub—station which is still there today. All Davy's old friends were gone; even my Grandmother had been laid low with a slight stroke. Eventually too Lisbeth died, and Davy became something of a recluse. From time to time he would be seen wandering down Polton Road to do his bit of shopping at Andrew Scott's grocery shop; always on the way back to his house with his bag of groceries there was the tell-tale bottle stuck in his coat pocket. Poor Davy, living a solitary existence, shut away from the world with only his bottle and his memories for company.

Then one bitterly cold winter's night our front door bell rang. There on the doorstep stood Davy, flanked on either side by Dr Young and Mr Jimmy Stone JP with Mr Curle from the Parochial Board Office bringing up the rear. Davy took a few faltering steps into the kitchen and announced that he had come to seek advice from his friend Alick (my Grandfather).

Memory Spill

He stood there with a Canadian fur-trappers hat on his head, the frosty rime which had been clinging to his beard melting and dripping down the front of his coat. Still the gentleman he removed his hat, his gaze searching for his friend Alick. Suddenly the lost look left the faded blue eyes; sitting in Grandpa's chair was my Uncle Harry who had inherited his father's build and looks. Here, thought Davy happily was his old friend Alick whose advice he sought. "They've come to take me to Rosslynlee, Alick, to be looked after. What do you think? Should I go with them?" My Uncle Harry played his part, took Davy's hands in his and said it was the best thing Davy could do. He had lived on his own long enough. And that was the last I saw of him; helped by his friends Jimmy Stone and Mr Curle he got into Dr Young's car. When it had disappeared up Polton Road I must confess there was a big lump in my throat.

He was well looked after at Rosslynlee during the remaining weeks of his life and died peacefully in his sleep. I feel certain that that other beloved Carpenter, the Man from Nazareth, would be there to welcome Davy with open arms when he arrived on the Heavenly Shore.

When the contents of Davy's house were sold off I attended the sale and for half-a-crown (12p) I bought a reasonably sound washing basket containing picture frames and glass and also one oil painting of a Knight in Shining Armour. I am firmly convinced that my Grandfather painted that picture and that Davy sat as the model for it, When I married and had a young family of my own the picture occupied a special place in our living room. The boys christened our two-and-sixpenny knight 'Uncle Fernando' and so he has remained down through the years. He is still with us gazing down on everyone benign and happy, his eyes always looking at you no matter where in the room you may be. A fitting reminder of my dear friend, Davy Reid the Lasswade carpenter.

Memory Spill

Index of the photographs

Memory Spill

Memory Spill

Page 195   The Lothian Family at the back door of 10
               Polton Road. Probably early 1890s.

Printed in Great Britain
by Amazon